A Will Too Live

by:

Colette D. Orr

Orr Novels Trademark

ISBN-13: 978-0692345450
ISBN-10: 0692345450

Website: http://www.orrnovels.wix.com/colettedorr
Facebook: https://www.facebook.com/orr.novels
Twitter: https://twitter.com/orr_novels
Email: orrnovels@yahoo.com

Thank You

This journey has truly been incredible! God, without you as my foundation, I know I would not be where I am today. Thank you for helping me fulfill my dreams!

To everyone who has bought my books, thank you so much! Your support has far exceeded my expectations.

To my sister, Cathy Nobles, and my brother, Council Orr, Jr, your desire for me to succeed has never gone unnoticed. Thank you for always being there. To my parents, Council Orr, Sr. and Mary Orr, I love that I have the best of both of you within me. It is truly a gift.

To Diane Owens, thank you for all the long nights and weekends you've spent editing my books. I understand and appreciate the sacrifice you make for me and I'm very thankful.

To Howard Carter, thank you for giving me the title for this book; I have thoroughly enjoyed writing it. May God bless you, Sheryl, and the entire Carter family.

To my children, Janessa, Katlyn, and Chaiden; you are my backbone. You give me fuel to keep going on days that I want to give up! Thank you for loving me unconditionally.

To all the children who know what it's like to live in an abusive home, I would like to say, you did nothing to deserve that and I pray that God heals ALL of your wounds (internally and externally). I dedicate this book to you. Much love!

Colette D. Orr

Chapter 1

"Can you believe I've put up with you for twelve whole years?" asked Patricia, as she looked over at her husband, Gilbert.

"Yup, and you've enjoyed every minute of it," he answered confidently with a cocky smile.

Patricia's eyes scanned the room and her facial expression suddenly became empty. "I want to have a baby, Gilbert. I want to be a mother," she said, slumping over and letting her arms dangle towards the floor.

Gilbert always hated when Patricia became depressed and emotional because he never knew how to respond. He really did want

to understand a woman's need to cry and

complain over things she could do nothing

about, but the concept was just too perplexing

for him to wrap his brain around. He lifted his

hand, deciding that maybe he should pat her on

her head or shoulder or something, and tell her

that everything would be okay, but somehow he

knew he would still get accused of being

insensitive. As he awkwardly thought of ways to

show his loving, caring, and sensitive side, the

doctor walked into the examination room.

THANK GOODNESS! Gilbert said with his

inside voice. *Now, I don't have to do all of that*

loving, sweet, and gentle ridiculousness!

Patricia rolled her eyes as if she was

reading his mind. "After twelve years, you

should know how to cuddle me, Gilbert," she

snarled.

The doctor gave them a weird look, but decided it was best not to ask what was going on.

"Hello again, Mr. and Mrs. Raine," the doctor said in a slightly agitated tone. "I was reading your records for today's visit and it says you've come to talk about having an In Vitro Fertilization?" he asked, with a baffled look on his face. "Do you even know what that is?"

Patricia let out a huge sigh. "I just want to have a baby, Dr. McGruff! Please just help me have a baby," she said, starting to cry.

The doctor looked over at Gilbert, giving him a signal to show some type of support towards his wife, but Gilbert gave the doctor an unsympathetic, *I wasn't the one who made her cry, so you better tap into your sensitive side and fix it* look.

The doctor awkwardly patted Patricia's hand, while giving Gilbert a mean glare, but Gilbert just smiled, not seeming to have a care in the world. That was until Patricia hit his arm.

"This is what I'm talking about, Gilbert. Why can't you just show me a little bit of affection?"

"I do show you—"

"On a more serious note," Dr. McGruff said, interrupting, and hoping to change the subject. "Mrs. Raine, I've been your doctor for a very long time and I know how much you want to have a child, but In Vitro Fertilization is to help people who are unable to get pregnant, not for those who are unable to carry a baby to full term. With this procedure, we take the man's sperm and the woman's eggs; we fertilize the eggs in our lab, place them back into the woman's body and hope that at least one will attach itself to the walls of the uterus. Mrs. Raine," he said, pausing. "You don't have a problem getting your eggs fertilized, your body is just unable to carry the baby to full term."

As heartbreaking as this was for Patricia to hear, Gilbert sat there with a big smile on his face as he pictured his masculine sperm hunting down and conquering Patricia's eggs. *I know my dogs can hunt,* he thought proudly.

When he was done with his thoughts of victory, he looked over at Dr. McGruff and Patricia, who were both staring at him like they wanted to kick him out of the room. Dr. McGruff took a deep breath and laid Patricia's records on his desk.

"Mrs. Raine, you've had fourteen

miscarriages in the last ten years, with your latest being as recent as six months ago. As I've told you several times before, there are plenty of adoption agencies out there. Please, please, please consider that as an option. You're only going to cause yourself more mental, physical, and emotional damage if you continue trying to carry a baby. I'm really sorry, but I just don't think it's going to happen, okay?"

When Dr. McGruff looked at Gilbert and Patricia, he realized his words may have been a bit hurtful. He tried his best to muster up a small smile to give them, but it was obvious that they were upset and no smile would soothe the harshness of the truth.

Patricia stared sternly at Dr. McGruff. She thought about all the years she had come to him and all the miscarriages they had shared together.

"My momma raised five kids by herself and I've never seen or heard her beg anybody for anything," Patricia said as tears rolled down her cheek.

Dr. McGruff gave her a side-eye frown, wondering where she was going with this story.

"She worked extremely hard every single day," Patricia continued, gazing up at a picture on the wall of an unborn baby forming in its mother's womb. "She always told us that God would provide. People in our community gave us food and clothes, and a lady even gave us a van so we wouldn't have to walk when we needed to go places. I watched my momma cry many days and nights as she told us how good God was to us. She would say, 'These gifts are hand-me-downs to other people, but they are miracles to us, and those people are angels from Heaven,' then she'd smile and give all of us hugs as we opened our new presents like it was Christmas morning."

Patricia looked away, then gazed back at the doctor.

"Now, Dr. McGruff, I don't know who or what you believe in, but all my life I have seen miracles and angels, and I'll be doggone if I'm going to start believing that God has lost His ability to help me have a child."

She leaped off the table.

"Thank you for your time, but we will be finding us another doctor who believes that God is able to work miracles," she added as she walked towards the door.

Dr. McGruff knew he should try to stop Patricia from walking out, but all of her miscarriages had taken a toll on him as well, and if the truth be told, he was tired of feeling like a failure for not being able to help her carry a baby to full term.

Patricia, just face it! You're not going to have a baby, so the sooner you and Gilbert realize this, the better off you will both be, the doctor thought, but he didn't say a word to Patricia as she walked out of the room. He looked over at Gilbert for a response, but Gilbert kindly just tipped his hat and gave him a cordial goodbye.

When they arrived at the car, Gilbert couldn't help but ask, "Patricia, do you really think we will have a baby one day?"

Patricia gazed out of her window. "Do you?" she asked.

"I believe I do," Gilbert answered.

"Me too," Patricia said, leaning her seat back and enjoying the rest of their ride back home.

Chapter 2

Several months passed, with Gilbert and
Patricia still adamantly trying to conceive a
child. Gilbert had just about given up on the
baby, although he was still enjoying the act of
trying to make one.

One day Patricia came into the kitchen
where Gilbert was sitting. She didn't say a
word; she just stood there staring at him. Since
he was really busy, he figured if he didn't
acknowledge her, she would just go away, but
there would be no such luck. When she saw
him glance at her out of the corner of his eyes,

she yelled, "GUESS WHAT?" with a gigantic grin on her face.

Danggit! She caught me, he thought.

"What?" he asked, wondering what was the deal with the huge grin.

"WE'RE PREGNANT!" she screamed.

"Now, hold on and calm down, Patricia. We've been here too many times before, so don't go getting yourself all worked up over nothing."

"But honey, I'm THREE months pregnant! THREE WHOLE MONTHS!"

"Is that supposed to be some magic number?"

"YES! I've never, ever made it to my three-month mark. Within a week of finding out that I was pregnant, I always had a miscarriage, but not this time, Gilbert. I've known for a whole month, A WHOLE MONTH!" she proclaimed. "I

A Will To Live

said, 'if I make it to three months, I will tell

Gilbert,' and here we are. This is our miracle

baby! I can feel it," she said, giving Gilbert a big

hug.

Gilbert stood there stiff as a board. The

thought of actually having a baby had put him

in a trance. Patricia let out a loud giggle.

"You've turned white as a ghost, honey! We

should name him Casper, after you," she said,

giggling even harder.

"Hmmm, Casper Raine...I kinda like the

sound of that," he said, coming out of his trance

and giving her an awkward kiss on her eye.

"Well, Casper Raine it is," she responded,

choosing to ignore how weird he became when

forced to show emotions.

As she twirled around the room rejoicing,

suddenly a gush of blood came running down

her legs, staining their brand new mint green

carpet.

"Oh, nooooooooo! Not again," Gilbert said.

"GET IN THE CAR!" he yelled. "I'm taking you to

the hospital."

"I'M NOT HAVING ANOTHER

MISCARRIAGE!" Patricia yelled back.

"Not now, Patricia. Get in the car!"

"I won't have another miscarriage. This

baby will live! I won't have another miscarriage!

This baby will live! I won't have another

miscarriage. This baby will live!" Patricia

repeated as they rushed to the hospital.

When they got there, they were rushed

into surgery. Dr. McGruff just so happened to

be the doctor on call that day. When he saw

them come in, he just shook his head.

Not again, he thought as he mentally

prepared himself for another miscarriage.

"I won't have another miscarriage. This baby will live!" Patricia whispered to the doctor.

He gave her a faded smiled, but there was something about her persistence and strength that made him want this baby to live more than any of the other fourteen times she'd miscarried. He gave her a gentle pat on the leg and continued to do everything he could to keep her from losing another child, but...he couldn't.

The baby expelled from her body and Dr. McGruff's head dropped to the floor. He slowly got up and gave Patricia his condolences for the fifteenth time. "I'm sorry, Mrs. Raine, really, I—"

"Dr. McGruff, look at this," the nurse interrupted. He turned around and looked at the monitor; there was another baby inside and this one was safely intact.

"Twins?" Dr. McGruff asked, letting out a huge laugh. "You were pregnant with twins!"

Gilbert and Patricia smiled.

The doctor examined the baby, and it seemed to be just fine, nestled safely in its embryo sac.

Dr. McGruff laughed. "I can't believe this. To be on the safe side, I want you to stay in the hospital tonight, okay?" he said to Patricia.

"Okay," she responded with a smile.

He couldn't help but smile back. "This may be a long road, Patricia. You may be on bed rest your entire pregnancy," he advised.

She smiled even brighter.

"This baby is going to live isn't he, Dr. McGruff?" she asked excitedly, with her husband standing there, just as eager as Patricia to hear the doctor's response.

"Well it's too soon to tell, but this one is definitely a fighter. That's for sure."

"We're going to name him Casper," she said, rubbing her belly.

"Oh, I see," said Dr. McGruff. "And what if it's a girl?"

"Then we're going to name her Casper," Gilbert chimed in with a sly grin.

"You two get some rest. I'll check on you in the morning," the doctor said, patting Gilbert on the shoulder, as if to praise him for his support towards Patricia.

The next morning, Dr. McGruff released them and they began their taxing journey as expectant parents. However, the next six months would be beyond problematic, with Patricia going in and out of the hospital with miscarriage scares. She eventually had to quit her job because the smallest amount of stress or pressure landed her in the emergency room. None of this mattered though, because as each month passed, they grew more and more confident that Casper would indeed live, and he did.

"It's a boy!" the doctor proclaimed on the evening of October 1st at exactly 7:40 pm, as Casper James Raine was born. "He weighs five pounds and four ounces," the nurse added.

"He's so tiny, is he okay?" Gilbert asked alarmingly.

"Yes, he's fine. Just a tiny little guy, that's all. His heart sounds great. All his vitals are good. He's perfect," Dr. McGruff said, just like he was the proud father. "Would you like to hold him?"

"Ummm, I don't know," Gilbert responded.

"Oh, he's a tough little fella; you won't hurt him."

"Uhhh, okay. Let me hold him then."

The nurse wrapped Casper in a blanket and placed him in his father's arms. Gilbert began to weep. He cried so hard that the nurse wondered if they should take the baby from him, but Dr. McGruff whispered, "I assure you, he's not going to drop that baby. Let them have their moment."

Dr. McGruff went over and gave Patricia a high five.

"We did it!" she said.

He had tears in his eyes.

"Yes, but you were the one who believed," he responded. "I'll check on you two in the morning, okay? And Congratulations!" he said, as he wiped his eyes and walked out of the room. The nurse asked Patricia if she wanted to let the baby lay up against her warm body, but she said, "No, I think he is perfect right where he is."

Chapter 3

Gilbert and Patricia loved Casper more than anything in the world. Patricia never returned to work after Casper was born. Neither she nor Gilbert could bear the thought of Casper being out of their sight and in the care of someone else. Gilbert was happy to be the sole provider for the family and Patricia was happy to be an at-home mom.

Each morning, she would lean over Casper's crib and sing an old Gospel song her mother used to sing at church.

♫ ♪ ♫ *If anyone should ever write my life story for whatever reason there might be* ♫ ♪ ♫

You'd be there between each line of fame and glory. Jesus is the best thing that ever happened to me ♫ ♪ ♫

Each time she'd sing that song, Casper would stare at her with his big brown eyes like he was soaking in every melody. As months passed, he started smiling whenever she sang to him, then he'd giggle and kick his legs until she was done. That was Patricia and Casper's daily bonding time, and it was hard to tell which one of them enjoyed it more.

Needless to say, as Casper grew older, he had the best of everything; the best clothes, the best shoes, and the best toys. On his first day of Kindergarten, Gilbert and Patricia cried like babies, humiliating poor little Casper in front of all his new classmates.

"I'll be fine. You can go," he said, pushing

both of them out of the classroom door.

Each day after school, all the kids in the neighborhood would make their way to Casper's house to play and to eat the popsicles Patricia had made for them. Gilbert and Patricia knew they would never try to have another child, so this was their way of giving Casper all the siblings he could ever hope for.

One day, all the kids were outside playing Red Light, Green Light, Stop, then out of nowhere, this little girl walked up and yelled, "Manny and Miguel, momma said get your butts in the house right now!" then she turned and walked back to the house, which was two doors down from Casper.

Casper had never seen her before. He just stood there, captivated by this feisty angel of light who showed up to make her demands, then turned away, not giving a second thought to how she just interrupted their game.

A couple of days later, Manny and Miguel returned to play. This time, the girl came with them. Sure, there were other girls there, and Casper thought of all of them as his neighborhood sisters, just like his parents taught him. However, whenever young Casper saw this little girl, sister was not what came to mind. She was different; she had spunk and although Casper didn't know what spunk was, he knew he liked it and he knew he liked her.

"What is your name?" he asked.

"Mariabella Alexandria Morales-Gonzalez, but you can call me Maria," she said, giving him a small grin. She was indeed the prettiest girl in the neighborhood, maybe even the universe. Her front tooth was slightly crooked, and for some reason, it was mesmerizing to Casper;

everything about her was mesmerizing to

Casper. He couldn't keep his eyes off of her, but

she didn't seem to mind.

"Are you gonna stand there and stare or

are we gonna go play?" she asked, running

towards the swing set. Of course, Casper ran

behind her. He'd be crazy not to.

As time passed, Casper discovered that as

beautiful as his sweet little Maria was, her home

life was far from it. Her mom was very abusive.

She would often get drunk and beat her

kids...and her husband. Maria's dad was

always too drunk himself to care. Casper's

house was Maria's escape from the torment

inside of her own home. It was where she could

go to imagine what life would be like with good

parents. She and her two brothers would all

hide in the closet, holding on to each other as if that would somehow save them from the agony of their mother's rage.

"Manny, get in the middle," Maria once said to her little brother. "Now let's all hold hands."

"Why do you want him in the middle?" Miguel, her older brother asked.

"Because his name means 'God is with us,' and we need God to be with us," she said frantically.

"My name means 'God is with us?" asked Manny.

"Yes, now pray," Maria instructed.

Each time they hid, they would put Manny in the middle, make him say a prayer, then do a pinky promise to never hurt each other. After their mom calmed down, they would come up with their own separate plans to one day escape the detestable world they lived in. Having Casper always made Maria's escape seem possible.

Casper's parents eventually embraced Maria as their own because she never wanted to go home. No one knew what was going on in her home, but she was very adamant when she would say to Casper, "I HATE LIVING THERE!"

He often tried talking his parents into letting Maria come live with them, but of course they blew it off as childhood puppy love.

One day, when Casper was eight, he was playing on his swing set while Maria was playing in the dirt beside him. He abruptly stopped his swing, looked over at Maria and said, "I'm gonna marry you and take you away from the boogeyman that lives in your house, okay?"

Maria smiled, showing off her crooked tooth that Casper loved so much.

"Okay," she responded, then they both went back to playing.

Each morning, while waiting on the school bus, Maria and Casper sat and talked. They sat together on the bus, they played together at recess, and they sat together again on the bus ride home.

As each year rolled by, Maria and Casper grew closer and closer. Of course, Casper noticed how Maria's body was starting to change. He tried very hard to not look at her in that manner, although he didn't quite know what "that manner" was. He noticed how extremely embarrassed she became when boys mentioned her budding boobs or her expounding hips and butt. Good thing Casper was always there to shut them up. Her brothers just sat there with repulsed looks on their faces wondering how anyone could find their sister attractive. It wasn't just an overprotective brother look, it was something else, but Casper could never put his finger on it. It didn't matter though, because he gladly took on the big brother role. He was happy to be Maria's mainstay and her protector. Besides, he was dealing with some unsettling puberty issues of his own, so it was best to just pretend none of it was happening. However, the one thing that did remain the same throughout Casper and Maria's childhood and adolescent years was how inseparable these two were. Well, that was until Casper's sixteenth birthday...

Chapter 4

♫ ♪ ♫ *Ding dong, ding dong,* ♫ ♪ ♫ the doorbell rang.

"Hey, what are you doing here?" Casper asked, opening the door and looking at Maria standing there in tight white shorts and a red t-shirt with silver glitter on it.

"I came to give you your birthday present," she said, walking in, taking off her shirt and throwing it across the room.

Casper squinted his eyes as glitter flew in his face. He looked at his childhood friend all grown up, attempting to give him a sexy pose in her black satin bra.

"Maria, what are you doing?" he asked, trying not to stare at her humongous boobs that had somehow snuck up on him over the years.

"I told you, silly, I came to give you your birthday present," she replied, taking off her bra and tossing it across the room with her shirt.

Casper's mouth dropped to the floor.

"Uuuuummmm, Maria, my parents— ummmm.....they will kill us if—"

"Shhhhh! Kiss me," she whispered, placing her lips on his.

Casper quickly obliged her request, although he had no idea what he was doing. He had never kissed anyone before, other than his mother and he was sure that was not the kind of kiss Maria was looking for. He slowly closed his eyes, because that's how they did it in the movies and he kissed Maria as best as he knew how.

She didn't seem to mind as he slobbered all over her face. They both moaned and groaned as she quickly unbuttoned his shorts, letting them fall in the middle of the living room floor. He took off her shorts and threw them across the room where her bra and shirt were, then threw his shirt in the opposite direction. They kissed all the way to his bedroom, which was only a few feet from the front door. They laid on his bed and he kissed her some more. His hand accidentally brushed up against her breast.

"Oh, I'm sorry," he said.

Maria gave Casper a weird look, with one eyebrow raised.

It's just that her boobs were so big that Casper was unsure of what to do with them, so he just stared at them.

"Stop looking at me and kiss me," she said seductively. "I'll show you what to do," she added.

They began to totally lose themselves in the moment, then suddenly, the doorbell rang and startled them both.

Casper looked down at Maria's body, which was ninety-five percent nude. The only thing left to take off was her black and blue laced panties, which Casper assumed was supposed to be a match to her black satin bra.

He looked towards the door, which, by this time, someone was aggressively beating on. He looked down at Maria again, then back at the door.

"Go ahead and answer it. It's probably important," she said disappointedly.

He contemplated on how important the person on the other side of the door could be in comparison to how important it was for him to remove those non-matching black and blue panties from Maria's body.

He huffed.

"What if it's your parents?" he asked fearfully, jumping off the bed and grabbing some shorts from his drawer.

"It's not them. My parents have been gone for two weeks. I have no idea when they'll be back."

"WHAT? Two weeks? I think it's illeg—"

"Who cares! I hope they never come back."

"Maria, don't say that. They are still—"

"BAM! BAM! BAM! BAM!" was the ferocious knock at the door again.

"Open the door, Casper!" Maria said in an aggravated tone.

Casper ran to the door, slightly opening it.

"Yes," he said suspiciously to the two male cops and a lady standing on his porch. One of the cops looked like he was fresh out of middle school. Casper wasn't sure if this was some practical joke.

"Hello, are you Casper Raine?" the older cop asked.

"Yes, what's going on?"

By then, Maria had thrown on one of Casper's t-shirts and shorts and had come to see who was at the door.

"What's going on?" she asked the cops, as if she lived there.

Both cops looked down at Maria's chest, noticing that she did not have on a bra.

"Sorry to interrupt what you two kids were obviously not supposed to be doing in here," the older cop said, looking back at Casper and nudging the young cop who was still staring at Maria's boobs.

The younger cop embarrassingly gathered his composure and looked up at Casper. The lady who was with them gave the young cop a subtle glare, trying not to show her aggravation.

"We have some bad news for you, Casper. Both of your parents have been killed in two separate automobile accidents and we are here to assist Ms. Holiday in getting you to your new home; she's with the Child Protective Services office," the older cop said, sorrowfully.

"How do you know who I am? I think you have the wrong person. You have the wrong family," Casper said intensely.

"NOOOOOO!" Maria screamed.

"This is a small town, Casper. We identified your parents at the accident scenes this morning. I'm really sorry, son," the cop said.

As Ms. Holiday tried to explain to Casper that he would have to go live with his grandmother, Maria was too busy still screaming for anyone to hear what was being said.

"Casper, I know this is hard for you, but can you go pack up a few of your things?"

"Where are you taking him?" Maria questioned.

"He has to go live with his grandmother until he turns the legal age of eighteen," said Ms. Holiday, trying to sound as sympathetic as possible.

"EIGHTEEN?" Maria screamed. "Please

don't take him away from me," she said,

wrapping her arms around Casper's neck and

holding on for dear life. "Please don't leave me,

Casper!"

Casper stood there in a daze, while the

cops pried Maria off of him, but in less than 30

minutes, they had somehow calmed the

situation enough to get Casper to put some

clothes in a suitcase.

"Once you get settled at your

grandmother's, she said she will bring you back

for the rest of your things," Ms. Holiday said to

Casper, who still seemed totally incoherent to

what was taking place.

"Please don't take him; he's all I got,"

begged Maria.

The cops grabbed Casper's bags and took

them to Ms. Holiday's car. Then they came back

to escort Casper. As they walked down the driveway, Casper stopped and looked back at Maria, who was still crying hysterically.

"Don't leave me. Please don't leave me," she said, sobbing uncontrollably.

"I'll come back for you," he mumbled, then he got into the car and rode off into the distance, leaving Maria with no safe place to call home anymore. But, little did Casper know, he would no longer have a safe place to call home, either.

Chapter 5

As Ms. Holiday pulled up to a small house in the deep woods of Tribuckle, Tennessee, Casper knew his life was about to change forever.

"C'mon in here, boy. Give yer grandma a hug," said this 4'9" little old lady, letting out a hearty laugh. "I haven't seen you since you were yay high," she added.

Casper's grandma and his dad had been estranged for quite some time. Casper remembered being around her when he was younger, but his memories were somewhat faded. Yet, when she gave him a hug, there was something familiar and comforting about her.

"Hey, grandma," Casper said, leaning in to return her hug.

Ms. Holiday got out of the car and immediately began explaining legal matters to Casper's grandma.

"Good lawd, this is a heap of papers ya got there," his grandma said to Ms. Holiday.

"Yes, ma'am. It's important that we get everything documented correctly."

Casper was sure his grandma didn't understand a word Ms. Holiday was saying, but she eagerly nodded her head in agreement, as Ms. Holiday guided her through each piece of paper.

After his grandma signed on every dotted line, he and his grandma said their goodbyes to Ms. Holiday and headed towards the front door.

"Are you hungry?" his grandma asked.

"Yes, ma'am. I'm starving."

"Okay, well let's get some food in that
stomach of yers."

Casper smiled at how funny his grandma
sounded. She reminded him of Granny from the
Beverly Hillbillies Show. He didn't understand
why his dad stopped talking to her; she had a
genuinely nice aura about her.

"Come on in," she said as she opened the
front door.

He walked inside and was immediately
greeted by two big, flying cockroaches.

"WHOA!!! WHAT WAS THAT?" he yelled,
almost running into the door.

"Them just roaches. You ain't never seent
no roach before, child? Lawdy, yer daddy got
you so sheltered."

Casper stopped dead in his tracks, refusing to take another step.

"Go on in, boy. Them roaches are more scared of you than you are of them."

"Nah, grandma. I don't think they're afraid of me at all," he said, trying not to act terrified.

"You can help yerself to whatever food I have. There's some ice cream in the freezer if you want some of that," she said.

Although ice cream was not Casper's idea of food, he felt pretty confident that there would be no roaches in the freezer, so he graciously accepted the offer.

"Ice cream, yum!" Casper said excitedly as he walked into the kitchen, immediately noticing a family of dead roaches in the corner. He let out a small gasp.

You gotta be kidding me, he thought.

He hesitantly got a bowl from the cabinet and pulled the ice cream from the freezer. When he opened the container, the ice cream looked like it had been melted, refrozen, and then freezer burned.

"Grandma, why does your ice cream look like this? It has icicles on it."

"Oh, child. Stop with yer foolishness. That ice cream is fine; it's just been in the freezer a little while."

There's no way in hades that mess is coming near my mouth, Casper thought.

Deciding against ice cream, he eased the container back in the freezer and the bowl back in the cabinet. He stayed in the kitchen a little while so his grandma wouldn't accuse him of being uppity.

There didn't seem to be much food in the house.

Maybe there's something in the pantry, he thought.

Just as he reached for the box of oatmeal pies, a mouse ran across the shelf.

"AAAAAHHHHHH!" Casper screamed.

"What you screaming like that fer, boy?" his grandma said, rushing into the kitchen.

"Grandma, you have rats too?"

"I ain't got no rats, boy; just a few mice here and there. Your daddy grew up in this house and he turned out just fine. It's a shame he ain't exposed you to real life."

Casper gave his grandma a blank stare.

"Grandma, do you think it's normal to live with rats and roaches?"

"Don't get smart with me, child. Me and

you got the same blood running through our veins, so don't come out here acting like yer better than yer grandma, ya hear?"

"I'm sorry. I really didn't mean it like that," Casper said regretfully. He sat down on the couch.

"Do you know what happened to my parents?" he asked.

She looked over at him like she was caught off guard. She came and sat down beside him.

"The social worker didn't tell you?"

"No, ma'am. All she said was they were both killed in two separate automobile accidents."

"Oh," his grandma said surprisingly. "Well, yeah. That's true. Yer mom got into an accident first. She was traveling down the main highway, going through a small town that had just put a traffic light up at one of the intersections. Well, a guy who lived down one of those back roads didn't notice that there was a new traffic light there. He had just gotten into a fight with his girlfriend, so he jumped in his truck to drive off and she jumped in with him. They continued to fuss and cuss all the way down the road and neither one of them noticed that the traffic light was red. He sped out onto the highway and ran right into your mom. Since his truck was so much bigger than her car, she flipped over several times and it crushed her inside. The guy's girlfriend got thrown from the car; she died as soon as she hit the concrete. I don't know how the guy is doing, but I heard he's pretty shaken up over the whole thing."

"So, what happened to my dad?"

"Well, since he worked as a dispatcher, he was the one who received the call when it came through on the emergency line. He immediately ran to his car and rushed to get to yer mom. They said he was driving almost a hundred miles an hour trying to get to the scene. A squirrel ran out in front of him, he tried to swerve, but lost control of the car. He hit a light pole and it pretty much split the car in down the middle. They said he died before the cops could even get there. Yer mom died in the ambulance, on the way to the hospital."

Casper just hung his head down in disbelief, but for some reason, he wouldn't allow himself to grieve.

"Okay. Please don't tell me anything else, grandma. I don't want to know," he said, looking like he had transformed his mind into another realm.

Tears rolled down his grandmother's face. She couldn't help but notice how empty Casper looked.

"I know yer hurting, son. It's okay to cry."

"I'm okay, grandma. I just wanted to know what happened, that's all. Thank you. I'm going to go to bed."

"Okay, suga. You can have the room down the hallway on the left."

"Okay, thanks."

She wanted to tell him what happened between her and his father. She wanted to explain how sorry she was and how much she regretted what she had done, but she knew he wasn't ready for that conversation. He had just lost both of his parents, for Pete's sakes. The least she could do was allow him time to grieve in whatever way he knew how.

Chapter 6

A few days passed and although the house was infested with rodents and pests, at least the critters seemed to have had a good understanding. The roaches mainly dwelt in the kitchen, while the mice made themselves comfortable in the bedrooms, with the exception of the one rebel mouse he saw in the pantry that day. The spiders, on the other hand, were running amok; their webs were everywhere.

"I can't live like this," Casper whispered as he laid in his bed staring up at a roach caught in a web.

The next week, his grandmother enrolled

him into high school. He was excited to finally begin his new life, desperately wanting to rid himself of the old one that had ended so tragically.

One day after school, his grandma was sitting at the kitchen table watching soap operas and peeling potatoes. When he walked through the door, of course he was greeted by the roach welcoming committee.

I don't know how much more of this I can take, he said to himself.

"What are you just standing around looking for?" his grandma said. "Put yer bags down and help me peel these potatoes."

If the truth was told, Casper would rather starve than eat anything from that kitchen.

He didn't understand why the social worker would drop him off there without seeing what environment he would be placed in. Just because his grandmother was the next of kin, doesn't mean she was a suitable parent.

"Do you know when they're gonna have my parents' funeral?" Casper asked his grandma.

She laid her knife on the table and said, "I was just wondering the same thing. Your Uncle Ray was supposed to be handling all of the funeral arrangements, but look like we would have heard something by now, though."

Casper grabbed a knife and helped his grandma finish peeling potatoes.

During dinner, he managed to fight off the roaches who were adamantly trying to take the potatoes off of his plate. However, whenever he tried to take a bite of his food, he almost vomited.

"I'm not in the mood for potatoes,
grandma. Do you mind if I just have a bowl of
cereal instead?"

"What I'd mind is you not wasting my
food, but go ahead. There's some Raisin Crunch
cereal in the pantry."

Casper grabbed a bowl and poured the
cereal in it. Just as he was about to add the
milk, he jumped up."

"Grandma! These raisins are moving!"

"What is the matter with you child? Them
raisins ain't moving."

His grandma looked over and saw a few
bugs crawling in his bowl.

"Oh," she said nonchalantly.

Casper threw up his hands.

"I can't live like this grandma," he said,
picking up the bowl and tossing the cereal in the

trash. "I'll just go to bed," he added, as he walked out of the kitchen.

That was the defining moment when Casper decided that school was the only place he would be getting his home cooked meals.

The next day, he gobbled down his cafeteria lunch like he hadn't eaten in months.

"How can you eat this stuff?" one kid asked. "It tastes like plastic solo cups with barbecue sauce on them."

Casper laughed.

"By the way, my name is Kris," the boy said. "Kris with a K."

"Okay, Kris with a K. I'm Casper."

"Like the friendly ghost?"

"Hahaha. Yeah, kind of. "

"How did your parents come up with a ghost's name?"

Casper laughed some more.

"Well, they had a very hard time having children, so when my dad saw that I might actually make it, my mom said he turned as white as a ghost, so they named me Casper."

"Umm, okay," Kris said, as if that wasn't justification enough to name your child after a ghost.

"Were you their only child?" Kris asked.

"Yeah. Before me, they had fourteen miscarriages and I'm actually a twin, but my twin died when my mom was three months pregnant. She was in and out of the hospital the entire time she was pregnant with me, but I made it. Needless to say, they never tried to have anymore."

"Hmmm," Kris said.

"Hmmm, what?" Casper asked.

"Out of sixteen kids, you were the only one that survived. You must have a will to live."

Casper laughed. "I never thought about it like that, but yeah, I suppose so," he replied proudly.

Kris and Casper immediately became best friends. Kris' home became to Casper what his home was to Maria; a safe haven, but Casper's grandma was not happy about him spending so much time away from her.

"Why do you have to be gone so much? There are crazy people out there and they hurt little kids," his grandma said in an overprotective tone.

"Grandma, I'm sixteen. I'm not a little kid anymore."

"Well, if yer here with me, I'll know that yer safe."

"Does this have anything to do with my father passing?" Casper asked, "because you don't have to worry about me. I'll be fine."

His grandma looked away.

"I don't even know if he and yer mother was given a proper burial. No one has told me nothing. I didn't even get to say bye," she said.

Casper sat down beside his grandma.

"I didn't either, grandma. I don't under—"

Just then Casper's uncle, Ray, came walking in the house like he owned it.

He looked over at Casper, without saying a word.

"Hey, momma. I hear we have a guest staying with us."

"He ain't no guest, Ray. He's family and family take care of each other, but I guess you wouldn't know anything about that, now would you?"

"Don't act like that, momma."

"It's true, Ray, but this time, I suggest you do what's right, or else."

Casper sat there, trying to decipher what they were saying. It was clear his Uncle Ray had done something his grandma didn't approve of. Casper knew there was something dark, wicked, and creepy about his uncle, but he never wanted to be around him long enough to find out what it was. His uncle came over a few times after that, and each time, it gave Casper chills.

Something else Casper noticed was how his grandma always clammed up when his uncle was around. She watched his every move as if she thought he was going to steal something. It definitely wasn't a natural mother/son interaction.

Occasionally, his uncle would ask him if he wanted to make some extra money, but his grandma would always cut the conversation off with, "No, he's just fine, Ray," before Casper could even respond.

One day, his uncle bumped into him, and brushed up against his body. Before Casper knew anything, he had balled up his fist and was ready to punch his uncle in the face.

"WHOA! Calm down! I'm sorry, nephew. I didn't mean to bump into you like that," his uncle said, apologetically.

"What's going on in here? You touching him?" his grandma asked, rushing from the kitchen into the living room where Ray and Casper were.

"I was just leaving," Ray said, grabbing his jacket and heading out the door.

Casper couldn't help but wonder if his dad's and grandma's estranged relationship had something to do with his uncle. He would make subtle hints to see if his grandma would tell him what really happened, but every time he asked, she would shut down, leaving Casper with so many unanswered questions.

Chapter 7

A few months passed and Casper had grown very weary of sharing his food, clothes, bed, and television with the roaches.

"Grandma, do you have any bug spray? I'll start killing a few roaches each day until they're all gone. Then maybe we can work on this mice mafia."

His grandma laughed as if he was joking, but the look on Casper's face told her that he wasn't. She had lived with mice and roaches all her life, and it sounded strange to hear someone suggest that they should be gotten rid of.

"I think there's some bug spray in the

laundry room," she responded solemnly.

Casper picked up a rusty can of bug spray sitting on the shelf.

"Grandma! We're gonna need way more than a one-third can of bug spray that expired three years ago."

His grandma laughed again as if Casper had suddenly become a stand-up comedian.

Again, Casper did not share in her laughter.

"We're gonna need to buy bug spray, mouse traps, and a broom to get these spider webs down," he said in a serious tone.

"I have a broom, child. You act like my house is nasty. I clean up every single day."

Casper looked over at his grandma like she was delusional.

To kill all of these bugs, I might have to

take out a loan, he thought.

He eventually did get a job and eagerly started helping his grandma with groceries, repairs and most importantly, pests and rodents.

Casper set mouse traps all over the house and by the end of the day, most of the traps actually had mice in them; some traps even managed to catch a few spiders and roaches, which was definitely a plus. After Casper started seeing a decrease in mice, he eagerly patched up the holes in walls.

"This should at least keep some of the mice out," he said.

"You're just a regular old handy man, huh?" his grandma asked.

"Not really, but I couldn't stand living like this anymore," he said harshly.

Casper saw the hurtful look his grandma had on her face. He felt really bad for what he said.

"I'm sorry. I didn't mean to hurt your feelings. It's just that—"

"No need to be sorry. I never realized how uncomfortable you must have been, until now. I've lived like this all my life. I've never even thought about there being a better way."

"Is that why dad never brought me here to see you?"

"NOOO!" his grandma snapped, which told Casper that perhaps he should change the subject, so he did.

"Grandma, if we keep working on the house, it's going to look brand new. I might even paint a little."

"Yes, it is," she said with a big grin on her

face.

As time went on, Casper completely turned his grandmother's house around. He even helped her start a garden, and oh, how she loved that garden. She spent most of her days tending to it! This worked out great for Casper because she didn't complain when he had to work or wanted to hang out at Kris' house. His grandma would be outside for hours, which is where she was one Saturday afternoon when his uncle stopped by unannounced like he always did.

"Where's momma?" he asked Casper.

"In the garden," Casper responded sourly.

"Oh, well then maybe I can have some time alone with you," his uncle said walking over towards Casper.

"Don't come near me, man."

"Relax, lil Gilbert. I'm family."

"Keep my dad's name out of your mouth, and if you're family then why didn't you tell me and grandma about my parent's funeral? I know they've been buried by now."

"Funeral? Ha! I'm not spending any money to bury them hags. I let them rot in the casket, just like they would have done for me."

"I'LL KILL YOU!" Casper yelled, grabbing a knife and running towards his uncle.

His uncle kicked him in the chest, but Casper managed to give him a good stab in his right leg, before he fell to the floor.

"You cut me! You shouldn't have done that, son," his uncle said with rage.

He punched Casper in the side of his face, almost causing him to black out.

Keep fighting, Casper, he told himself.

He was hitting his uncle as hard as he could with every object he could get his hands on; lamps, books, plates, cups, shoes; everything was flying everywhere, but his uncle was way too strong for him and he eventually beat Casper until he couldn't fight anymore. Casper laid helplessly on the floor in his own puddle of blood.

"Now, you're just like I want you," his uncle said, pulling Casper's pants down, then unbuckling his own.

"GET OFF HIM! GET OFF HIM! I WON'T LET YOU DO THIS AGAIN!" Casper heard his grandma yell. He could sense that she was hitting his uncle with some object, but he himself had no more fight in him and was barely holding on for dear life.

After his grandma beat his uncle off of

him, she called the ambulance.

"I'm so sorry, Casper," he heard her say, weeping uncontrollably as his uncle ran out of the door. "I'm such a terrible grandma and I'm so very sorry."

Casper had only caught bits and pieces of what his grandma was saying, then he lost total consciousness.

The ambulance crew rushed him to the hospital, and did their best to save him. He didn't seem to have much life or blood left in him. They managed to get him to the hospital, but it wasn't looking good. They continued to do everything in their power to save him, even if they felt that he was a loss cause.

His grandma was frantically pacing in the waiting room, hoping and praying that Casper would be okay. When the cops came up to ask her what happened, she was so delusional that nothing she said made sense. She kept crying and crying and shouting and shouting.

"I PROMISED I WOULDN'T LET THIS HAPPEN TO HIM AGAIN! PLEASE SAVE MY GRANDSON! I'M A HORRIBLE PERSON! I SHOULD HAVE TESTIFIED! I SHOULD HAVE LET THEM LOCK HIM UP! I DIDN'T WANT TO LOSE MY SON. WHAT WAS I SUPPOSED TO DO? I TRIED SO HARD TO KEEP THIS FROM HAPPENING! I TRIED SO HARD!"

Several times, the cops attempted to calm her down, but it was no use. She kept going on and on about how everything was all her fault, but none of it was coherent enough for the cops to consider it a statement for what had happened to Casper. Then right there in the waiting room, she had a heart attack and died in the arms of the cop, and with her, also dying

were many, many vile family secrets.

Chapter 8

A few days passed, with Casper still lying in the hospital, unconscious. They placed him on life support, but outside of the machine, there was truly no sign of life in his body. Casper's friend, Kris, visited him every day, but since he wasn't family, he could not make any medical decisions for Casper.

Days later, the hospital was finally able to make contact with Casper's next of kin, his Uncle Ray, who seemed totally distraught that this had happened to his favorite nephew.

"My nephew has been suffering in the

hospital a whole week and you guys are just contacting me? This is unbelievable!" said Ray, staring furiously at the doctor.

"Sir, we've tried to reach you every day, since the first day he was admitted, but we were unable to. Now that I have you here, there's something else I need to inform you of," the doctor said, pausing. "I'm sorry, but your—"

"Oh, lawdy, my nephew is dead! Please don't tell me my nephew is dead," his uncle said, pretending to cry. "Where's my momma? Is she here with him? I know she must be as horrified as I am. Where is she? I need to see her."

"Sir, the other reason we've been trying to reach you is because your mom died in the waiting room a week ago."

"A WEEK AGO?" he screamed. "Why nobody told me?"

The doctor did his best to maintain his composure. He gave a slight blank stare at the wall, then said, "Again, we tried numerous times to reach you, but we were unable to."

"Well, I had to go out of town for a few days," he snapped, "but that's no excuse for y'all to not contact me. I should have been told about my momma. Where is her body?"

"Her body was turned over to the hospital's mortuary. I'll be glad to walk you down there as soon as we're done here. I'm very, very sorry for your loss."

"I can't believe y'all did this to my mother! You will be hearing from my lawyer," he added.

By that time, the doctor was losing his patience and refused to spend any more time on this foolish conversation.

"So, the reason I asked you to come down

here is because I'm really not sure if your nephew is going to make it through the night. He's been beat up pretty badly. He's bleeding from his brain as well as other internal organs. We've done all we can do for him, but he's just not responding. Even if he somehow survives this tragedy, he will probably never return to normality as he once knew it. Since you are his next of kin, I need you to consider removing him from the life support machine in the morning."

"In the morning? I just can't do this! I can't do this!" his uncle said, wiping dry tears from his eyes.

"On a side note," the doctor said, lowering his voice. "Do you have any idea who did this to him?"

"Nooooooo!" his uncle snapped, switching from distraught to abrasive. "I was told he's a leader of one of the local gangs around here. He's always been a troubled kid. His childhood was very rough, ya know? His parents were horrible to him. I did what I could as his uncle, but as much as I love him, it may be best for the Lord to take him on home tonight. Just go ahead and pull the plug, Doc. Put him out of his misery."

The doctor gave him a weird look.

"I like to give family members at least 24 hours to think everything over."

"Well, those gang members will probably shoot up this entire hospital looking for Casper. For the safety of the town, you may wanna just pull the plug and get it over with," he said, as he began his fake river of tears. "Please, don't make me suffer all night with the thought of losing another beloved family member. Please,

Doc, just put him out of his misery now."

"I understand, but it is the hospital's policy that we wait 24 hours. We do not take these types of decisions lightly. Just think it over and come by tomorrow, okay? Oh, by the way, the cops were looking for you earlier this week to gather evidence on what happened to your nephew. You may want to stop by and see them—"

"Them rascals already saw me! Dirty, stank cops! They found me the next day after it happened."

"I thought you said you didn't know your nephew was in the hospital."

"Oh," his uncle said nervously. "I didn't. What I was trying to say was there is no need for me to go see them because they will probably find me tomorrow, now that I'm back in town."

"Uhhhh, okay. Well, I'll see you tomorrow morning. And I'll be honest with you, Casper will probably pass within a few minutes of us disconnecting the life support machine, so please prepare yourself for that, okay?"

"Can I see him?" his uncle asked.

"Sure, but he's in pretty bad shape," the doctor said, giving Casper's uncle a pat on his shoulder.

Casper's Uncle Ray went into his room. When he looked at him he knew Casper wouldn't live through the night, which made it even better that he wouldn't have to make the decision to pull the plug in the morning.

"Look at you! Laying up here! I don't even recognize who you are. This is what happens when you try to go up against me. I hope you've learned your lesson, son. You should have just let me do what I was going to do and you would still be alive, but you're so darn stubborn! Just like your father. I hated that man!" his uncle said. Then he leaned over and whispered in Casper's ear, "Tomorrow, if you live to see tomorrow, they're going to pull the plug on you and you will die. I wish tomorrow was tonight, and oh, by the way, your grandma is dead and that's all your fault, too! That's okay though because tomorrow all your inheritance will come to me. Boy, I wish you could see this nice suit I just bought myself with all the cash momma got from your trustee fund. I had no idea my brother was rich. Being next of kin is a beautiful thing," his Uncle Ray said as he let out a hearty, evil laugh. "Goodbye, nephew. Sleep tight."

Little did he know, Casper's friend, Kris

was in the bathroom and he heard the entire

conversation. Kris stepped out of the bathroom

and looked Casper's uncle right in the face.

Uncle Ray jumped, but Kris didn't say a word.

He just stared at him like he was trying to

refrain from killing him. As Uncle Ray waited

nervously for Kris' reaction, a nurse came into

the room to check Casper's monitor.

Chapter 9

"Did I interrupt something?" the nurse asked, noticing the malicious look Kris was giving Casper's uncle.

"Noooo! Come on in," Uncle Ray said. We weren't talking about anything important."

"Can I use your phone to call the police?" Kris asked, still staring Uncle Ray down like he wanted to devour him.

"Uh, are you talking to me?" she asked.

"Yes," he said, not taking his eyes off of Uncle Ray.

"Is something wrong?" she asked Kris.

"Yes, this—"

"NO! Nothing is wrong," Uncle Ray interrupted.

"Yes, there—"

"Little boy, I don't know who you are, but I suggest that you don't go putting your nose in business where it doesn't belong," Uncle Ray said threateningly.

"Or you will do what? Put me on my death bed like you did Casper?" Then he turned to the nurse and said, "This guy here, Casper's next of kin who was supposed to love Casper so much, is the one who did this to him."

The nurse squinted her eyes at Kris and sympathetically said, "I'm really sorry about your friend, honey, but it has been reported that this was a gang-related incident."

Kris looked at her like she was crazy.

"You seem like a sweet kid," she

continued, "So if you're also a part of this gang, I pray that you get out now."

"GANG?" Kris shouted. "Casper is not in a gang, so you can send that lie back to where it came from. Casper is afraid of cockroaches and mice; no gang is going to let him in their group."

The nurse looked as if she was starting to believe him.

"He is in a gang. Don't try to defend him," Uncle Ray chimed in like this was just the thing he needed to discredit Kris.

"That's a lie! I assure you, Casper was not in any gangs."

"Don't tell me you believe this infidel," Uncle Ray said to the nurse. "And why is he in here anyway? I didn't authorize my nephew to have any visitors. This kid is not even family."

As things began to escalate between Kris

and Uncle Ray, the nurse began to get a little

frightened. She slowly started taking steps

towards the emergency button next to Casper's

bed. She didn't want to make any sudden

moves because at this point, she didn't know

what to believe.

"I'm sorry, but I'm going to have to ask

both of you to leave the room," the nurse said

calmly.

"Good, because I need to go make a phone

call," Kris said angrily.

"Well, I'm not going anywhere! There's no

way a lying gang banger is going to come in

here, trying to intimidate me." Then Uncle Ray

said to the nurse, "When you came through the

door, the reason it was so tense was because he

had just asked me for twenty dollars and when I

told him I didn't have it, he threatened to rob

me."

The nurse let out a gasp.

"Now he's trying to act like he's not in a gang," the uncle continued. "Matter of fact, I'm the one who should be calling the cops. That's why I was—"

Before Uncle Ray was able to finish his sentence, out of nowhere, Kris seemingly leaped over Casper's bed, across the entire room, ran along the wall, onto the night stand and socked Uncle Ray right in the nose.

"HELP! HELP! We need help in here," the nurse yelled.

The uncle grabbed Kris and threw him up against the wall, then as the nurse decided to run out of the room to get help, Uncle Ray grabbed her and slammed her on the floor. Kris ran and hopped on his back, hitting him with whatever he could, but Kris was no match for Uncle Ray. He threw Kris into the door. As they were scuffling, the nurse started crawling towards the door again, screaming, "WE NEED HELP IN HERE! SOMEBODY! HELP!"

Uncle Ray grabbed her legs, then pushed Casper's monitor over onto the nurse. Kris started yelling for help and Uncle Ray threw his shoe at him to shut him up, but Kris ducked. He tackled the uncle, who was already lying on the floor, trying to keep the nurse from calling for help. The workers at the desk down the hallway got a system notification that Casper's monitor was unplugged, so they ran in to see what was going on.

"CALL SECURITY! CALL SECURITY!" the nurse yelled when the others came running through the door. Within seconds, three security guards were in the room. They pulled Kris off of Uncle Ray.

"He did this to Casper," Kris yelled to the security guards, who looked over at the nurse for confirmation.

"Yes, I believe he did as well," the nurse said, still huffing and puffing. They handcuffed the uncle, then the nurse said, "Before y'all take him away, can I say one thing?"

"Sure, what is it?" one of the security guards asked.

"The nurse looked over at the uncle standing there with an evil smirk on his face. She walked up to him and slapped him as hard as she could.

"That's for pulling my hair out! I paid a hundred dollars to get this weave in yesterday, now I've got to go back and get it redone!" she said with a serious look on her face.

The security guards and the rest of the staff couldn't help but laugh. She was the head nurse, but also the one who kept the group laughing throughout the day.

"Are you gonna let her hit me like that?" the uncle asked the guards.

"Yeah, I believe we are," one guard said, laughing.

"Y'all go ahead and take this fool out of here, before I slap him again for messing up my makeup."

As the security guards hauled the uncle off, the nurse reached over and gave Kris a hug.

"Are you really not in any gangs, honey?"

"No, ma'am. My momma is a lot like you and she would kill me."

"Good!" she said laughing. "Now go on

home, but I need you to ask your mom if you can come back tomorrow, because your friend is scheduled to be taken off of life support at nine o'clock in the morning and I know he would love to have you here when he returns home to meet his maker," she said, giving Kris another hug. "I'm so sorry this happened to him. Really, I am, but he's going to be in a better place, she added."

Kris just stood there crying on her shoulder like he had known her for years.

"He's my best friend. Please don't pull the plug. Give him another chance. He's the only child that made it out of fifteen miscarriages. Just give him a chance; I know he can pull through."

All the nurses stood there with tears in their eyes.

"I'm sorry, baby, but there is nothing we can do. Just try to come early, so you'll have time to say good-bye, okay?"

Kris took a deep breath. "Okay, I'll see you in the morning," he said, wiping a tear.

"Okay, in the morning," she replied, as Kris walked towards the door.

Chapter 10

The next morning, Kris arrived early just as the nurse advised.

"Hey, young man, I see you made it," she said.

"Yeah, my parents are here with me too," he said, pointing to the couple standing down the hallway.

"That's great! Tell them to come on down."

"Well, I would like to have a minute alone, so I can talk Casper into coming back," he said, giving her a hopeless smile.

"Okay, well you go do that then," she said smiling back.

"Hey! Casper the ghost rider," Kris said, as he pushed Casper's room door open, trying to make light of what was about to happen. He pulled a small stool up to Casper's bed. He looked at his best friend laying there lifeless. He couldn't imagine life without him around. Kris dropped his head on the bed and he began to cry like a baby.

"You gotta wake up, man! They're gonna pull the plug on you in one hour! One hour! I know you're a fighter, so why won't you fight, Casper? Fight, man! You were the only child who made it, remember? I know you have a will to live and I need you to live more than I've ever needed anything. You gotta live, man! Live, Casper...live!" Kris said. He sat there repeating the words, "Live, Casper...live! Live, Casper...live!"

Over and over, he repeated it.

Soon, the doctor came in with several nurses, and Kris' parents walking cheerlessly behind them.

Kris knew he was about to say goodbye to his friend and he just wasn't ready.

The doctor explained that Casper would probably die within a few minutes of the plug being pulled. He also explained that typically if you're not family, you would not be allowed to witness this procedure, but giving the horrific circumstances, he would make an exception. Then he thanked Kris' parents for being with Kris during this time. "He's been up here every day since Casper was admitted. I can't think of a better friend that I'd rather have by my side," the doctor said. His loyalty is definitely a credit to his upbringing and for that, you two should be very proud. You have a fine young man. I'm sure he will do well in life." Then he looked at Kris and said, "Casper needs you to be strong. He's going to a better place, so don't worry about him. You continue to do the right thing on his behalf. Continue to show other kids what true friendship is. I'm telling you, son, some people live to be a hundred years old and never experience the beauty of friendship. To have someone in your corner that you can trust and depend on through the good times and the bad, someone who will stand by your side when you need them the most; that is what friendship is all about. It is a gift that money will never be able to buy, and Casper has that gift in you," the doctor said, patting Kris on the knee. By the time the doctor was done with his speech, there wasn't a dry eye in the room. The nurse was passing tissues around like candy. Even the doctor had to wipe a tear or two.

"Okay," the doctor said. "I think we should go ahead and get started. And remember, son," he said, looking up at Kris again. "Hearing is the last sense that leaves the body, so let's just hope he's heard some of these words today. Then he will leave this world knowing how loved he really was."

Kris smiled as if that had given him some kind of comfort. "Thank you," Kris responded, as the doctor gave the nurse the go ahead to pull the plug.

The nurse despondently did as she was told. She knew she wasn't supposed to become attached, but she wanted Casper to live...for Kris' sake if nothing else.

"Three....two....one," the nurse said as she

removed Casper from life support. Everyone let out a sigh, then silently watched the monitor to see if any sign of life would appear on the screen.

Instead of the spaced out "Beep...beep...beep...beep" that they once heard when they entered Casper's room, all they could hear now was death. Not just any kind of death, but a long, antagonizing sound of beeps angrily pressed together into a machine that knew no beginning or no end.

"Beeeeeeeeeeeeeeeeeeeeeeeeeeeeeeeeeeee..." was all they heard. Everyone knew what this sound meant. This reassured them of what they didn't want to know; that Casper was gone.

Kris dropped his head to the floor and his parents wrapped him in their arms while he wept like a baby.

The doctor and the nurses stood there, giving them a minute to mourn, but it was evident that Kris would need more than just a minute.

"Beep....beep....beep...."

"What is that?" Kris asked the doctor and the nurses who were all gathered around Casper's monitor.

"Beeeeeeeeeeeeeeeeeeeeeeeeeeeeeeeeeeeeeeeee..."

"Beep....beep....beep....beep"

"PLUG THE LIFE SUPPORT BACK UP! PLUG IT UP!" The doctor yelled, as the nurses rushed over to plug Casper back up to the life support machine.

"I can't believe this! I think he's trying to breathe on his own!" the head nurse said, smiling.

"What is going on?" Kris asked again.

97

"It's too soon to tell, but it looks like Casper isn't ready to die yet," the doctor said, as he performed other tests on Casper.

"Draw some blood for me, let's check his vitals..." he said, continuously shouting out a variety of orders for the nurses to perform on Casper. Kris and his parents sat quietly waiting to see if Casper was going to make some sort of movement.

Everything was moving so fast, and all the nurses were doing so much that Kris couldn't make heads or tails of whether he should have hope or not. He didn't ask any more questions, he just put his hand on Casper's arm, and repeatedly said, "Live, Casper...live!"

His parents heard him and decided to join in, "Live, Casper...live!" they said, placing their hands on Casper's arm too.

"Unplug the life support. I want to see if we can get him to breathe on his own again," the doctor said.

Although hearing those words made Kris nervous, he continued to encourage Casper to live.

"Uhh! Uhhh!" they heard coming from Casper.

"I think he's trying to breathe!" one nurse yelled.

This sound from Casper put all the nurses and the doctor in even more of a tailspin. They were all running around, doing everything under the heavens to try to get him to come back.

While Kris' head was still face down on Casper's bed, he suddenly let out a yell.

"Casper moved! I felt him move!"

Kris jumped up and there Casper was with

slightly opened eyes looking around like he was clueless as to what was going on, but it didn't matter because his eyes were still open and that meant he was alive.

"His eyes are open! His eyes are open!" Kris yelled and everyone rejoiced. The nurse unplugged the life support machine again.

This time, all they could hear was the beautiful sound of perfectly harmonized beeps. It was music to their ears.

"He's alive!" the doctor said.

No one was happier to hear those words than Kris! He held up Casper's hand and gave him a high five!

"I knew you couldn't leave me, man!" Kris said, still rejoicing.

Kris could only make out a small crack of a smile from Casper because of all the tubes still stuck down Casper's throat, but to Kris, that was way more than he could ever hope for.

Chapter 11

As time passed, Casper grew a little bit stronger each day. He still couldn't speak that well, but he could speak. Nor could he walk very well, but he was beginning to take a few steps. Casper was nowhere near one hundred percent, not even near fifty percent, but he was definitely alive; anything was an improvement from where he had been.

When the doctor made his rounds with all the patients each day, he would say to Casper, "I was wrong about you and I'm so glad."

Casper always let out a small laugh as

best as he could. He would stutter, "Me too."

One day, the doctor said to Casper, "You have a true and loyal friend in that Kris fella, ya know? I believe the only time he wasn't here was when he had to be in school. Other than that, he was right here talking to you like you could understand everything he was saying."

"Really?" Casper said surprisingly.

"Do you remember anything he said to you?" the doctor asked out of curiosity.

"No, not really, but it was the strangest thing, because several times I remembered walking towards this really, really bright light and out of nowhere this huge angel would come and walk beside me. We would mostly just walk in silence, then out of nowhere, a big number three would come out in front of us to let us know that we were three feet from the light, then the angel would place his wing over my body,

shielding me from the light, and he would

whisper, 'Live, Casper...live!' and that's all I

remember. Isn't that weird?" Casper asked.

"No, son! That's not weird at all because

those were the exact words your friend spoke to

you."

"Kris said that to me?"

"Yep! He sure did. He was your angel,"

the doctor said laughing.

"Hahahaha! You don't know Kris. He's no

angel," Casper refuted, "But what about that big

number three? What was that all about?"

The doctor laughed, "Well, I'm not a dream

interpreter, and I really shouldn't talk religion

with my patients, but if you want to know my

personal opinion, I will surely give you that."

"Definitely," Casper responded eagerly.

"Well, I think it would do you some good to read up on what different numbers mean in the Bible and the different scenarios God uses those numbers in. For instance, when Jesus died on the cross, why were there two more guys with him, making it a total of three people who died on the cross that day? Why did Jesus remain in the grave three days before he arose? Why does God represent himself as a trinity; three in one?"

"Wow!" Casper said. "You're right!"

"And why did Jonah spend three days in the belly of a whale? And why were there Three Wise men that went to find baby Jesus? Why three? Why not two? Do you want to know something else about the number three?"

"Yes, what?"

"Jesus' ministry on this earth only lasted three years, but, again, I'm just a doctor, not a

Bible scholar, but I think it goes without saying that there is something very special about this number three. Some say the number three represents divine perfection. I don't know, but it's obvious that it represents something."

"That's for sure! I had no idea Kris was an angel," Casper said, chuckling.

"Angels come in many disguises, Casper. And yes, some are even disguised as our best friend. That's why you have to be careful how you treat people. Don't take advantage of people who are good to you and don't abuse people's kindness, because they just might be sent from heaven," the doctor said, smiling. "Okay, buddy, I'm way over my time here. I'll come back in the morning to check on you."

"Hmmm," was the only response Casper could give. He was consumed with trying to picture if his angel had Kris' face, but he couldn't remember anything but those big wings hovering over him and those words, 'Live, Casper! Live!"

Casper was truly puzzled by this entire conversation with the doctor. He needed to find out more about this number three.

"Try to get some rest," the doctor recommended while still writing notes on Casper's chart. We will keep you in ICU for a little while longer and will continue to monitor your health. If you heal properly and get stronger, we will move you into a regular room, then begin your mental and physical therapy to get you back on your feet, okay?"

"Okay," said Casper.

As each day passed, Casper grew stronger and stronger. He was far from a vegetable. His determination to fully recover was envied by all

of the hospital staff and soon he healed well

enough to go home. Except he didn't have a

home to go to.

"Hi there, Casper," the social worker, Ms.

Holiday said, walking into his room.

"What are you doing here?" he asked,

sitting straight up in his bed.

"Well, we've been monitoring your health

over the past few months and the doctor thinks

you're ready to be released."

"Umm hmmm," Casper responded as if

that still didn't explain why she was there.

"I'm here to take you to your new home,

Casper."

"My new home? What new home?"

"Until you turn eighteen, we cannot legally

allow you to raise yourself. We have a great

family that's willing to let you come live with them until you graduate high school."

"But I'm seventeen now and I'm graduating in six months. Why can't I just live in my grandma's house?"

"I'm sorry, Casper. The law does not deem you of legal age to take care of yourself."

Casper had spent several months in the hospital recovering, which sucked dry all of the inheritance his dad left for him, minus the money his uncle splurged when he thought Casper was going to die.

Casper was thoroughly dreading going to another family. "Can I call my best friend's mom to see if I can live with them?"

"Yes, but since you are in the care of the courts, we will have to speak with them, and do some paperwork and things of that nature to make sure they can provide a suitable living environment for you."

"Are you kidding me? Did you even bother to go into my grandmother's house before you dumped me on the curb? Let me just tell you, that was not a suitable living environment. Then I was exposed to my pedophile uncle who tried to kill me. The least you can do is allow me to stay with people who love me."

"I'm very sorry about what happened to you. We feel that it is always in the best interest of the child to be in the care of family if at all possible. When we contacted your grandmother, she was so very happy about you coming to live with her that I just knew it would work out great, but I was wrong. I failed you, and I'm terribly sorry," she said. "Go ahead and call your friend's mom and I'll see what I can do."

Casper eagerly called Kris and asked if he could move in with them until he graduates.

"My mom said of course you can, but we just left town to go up to Michigan for my granddad's funeral. He had a heart attack last night and died. My mom is pretty torn up about it. We'll probably be gone for a week, but she said the key is under the side doormat. Go ahead and make yourself at home," said Kris.

"Man, thank you! I'm so happy I don't have to go live with strangers."

"What? What do you mean?"

"Man, the social worker is here and she's trying to take me to some foster home. I just can't do the stranger thing again."

"That's crazy! No, you can definitely come live with us. Just ask her if you can stay in the hospital until we come back."

"Okay, I will."

"Okay, later, and I'm really sorry about your grandpa."

"Thanks, it's okay. He was ninety-eight. He had a good life."

"Wow! I guess so! I'll call you later and tell you what the social worker says."

"Alright. Bye."

"Later."

Casper enthusiastically told Ms. Holiday what Kris' mom said, but she wasn't at all impressed with that plan.

"Casper, I can't allow you to go get a key from under someone's doormat and live there by yourself until they return from Michigan who knows when. I want to help you, but I'll get fired for going along with that plan."

"Well, I'll just check myself out of the

hospital and you don't have to know where I'm going."

"No, can do, either!"

"How about I just stay here until they return then?"

"Well, that idea wouldn't be so bad, except there is no more money in your trust fund to allow you to stay here. The money ran out over a week ago, but people have donated money to let you stay this long. Now, that money has run out as well. You're in good health, though, so it's really time for you to leave the hospital. Besides you have a great family who has willingly opened their doors to take care of you. Can you just give it a try?"

"I don't want to go live with anyone else that I don't know."

"How about you just stay with them until

Kris' parents return, then I'll set up a time to meet with his parents and we'll get the paperwork started to make them guardian over you until you turn eighteen. Is that a deal?"

"Yeah, I guess one week with strangers can't hurt," Casper said, as he packed up his things, said goodbye to all the nurses, and headed out the door.

"I know you're not leaving without giving me a hug," the head nurse said, running out the door after Casper.

"Oh, no, ma'am. I looked for you, but I didn't see you."

"Take care of yourself, son. It is truly a miracle that you are even here. From what I've heard, the devil has tried to kill you several times, but you have continued to escape, you little rebel," she said smiling.

As she kept talking, Casper began thinking about all the near-death experiences he's had so far. *That is crazy,* he thought.

"Are you listening to me?" the nurse said, interrupting Casper's deep thoughts.

"Ummm, yes," he responded, but it was obvious that she had been standing there a while, imparting words of wisdom to him while he was deep in another world. To keep her from continuing on, he gave her a quick hug, promised to keep in touch and jumped in Ms. Holiday's car.

"The Stevens family are good people, Casper. You'll like them," Ms. Holiday said as they drove down the highway. "They have been wanting to take in another child for quite some time now."

"But I'm not a child. I'm a grown man!"

"Not quite, Casper. Please try to be thankful that someone is willing to take a seventeen-year-old under their roof. Most people don't want kids past the age of seven.

Casper took a deep breath.

"Okay," he said, trying to sound appreciative while silently enduring the rest of the ride to his new home.

Chapter 12

When he got there, everything seemed perfect. He immediately noticed how no roaches came to the door to greet him; he was very excited about that. Although he would have fought off a million roaches if he could have his grandmother back and his parents too, for that matter.

Mrs. Stevens quickly took Casper's mind off of his troubled past with some homemade brownies.

"Katherine's brownies are the best," Mr. Stevens said to Casper about his wife.

She handed Casper a brownie and he took a bite.

"Wow, these are delicious!" he said, *although not as delicious as my mom's,* he wanted to add, but didn't. He could tell they were putting forth a special effort to make sure he felt at home, and he did.

"In a couple of days, we will start your homeschooling, okay?" Mrs. Stevens said to Casper.

"Homeschooling? I'm not going back to my old school?"

"I'm afraid not, honey. That school is almost two hours away. We've hired a teacher to come by for a few hours each day to help you get back on track. We're not sure that you'll be able to graduate this year since you've been out for so long, but we're definitely gonna try and get you there, alright?"

"But, I thought I was only supposed to be here a week?"

"A week?" Mr. and Mrs. Stevens said, giving him a strange look.

Casper didn't bother to explain the agreement he made with Mrs. Holiday. He just hung his head down in disappointment. He couldn't believe he wouldn't be hanging out with Kris at school anymore, and since his cell phone had mysteriously disappeared, there was no way to call and let Kris' parents know where to come pick him up when they returned from the funeral.

However, to Casper's surprise, he had a foster sister to help keep him company; her name was Shayla. Shayla was tall and slender with long, coarse, curly hair. She looked like she was mixed with African American and some other race.

Maybe she's from the Virgin Islands, or Cuba or—oh, who knows, but she sure is pretty, Casper thought.

She looked nothing like Mr. and Mrs. Stevens. They weren't even the same race, so it didn't take much for Casper to assume that she was also a foster child.

Mr. and Mrs. Stevens were both very attractive. They looked to be in their early sixties, but it was obvious that they had broken quite a few hearts in their day. They seemed like really wonderful people, but for some reason, Shayla never seemed happy around either of them.

"What's your story?" Casper asked Shayla one day when Mr. and Mrs. Stevens had gone across town to visit friends.

"What story?" she replied in a short-tempered tone.

"Where are your real parents?" he asked.

She let out a sarcastic chuckle.

"What makes you think I'm not living with my real parents?"

"Are they your parents?"

"No way!" she said, rolling her eyes with one foot propped up in the chair, and clipping her toenails.

"Why did you say it like that? They seem like really nice people."

"They are not my real parents, okay?"

"Why are you so touchy, Shayla? Tell me your story," Casper inquired again.

"Why do you want to know? So you can feel sorry for me?"

Casper gave her a weird look.

"I don't even feel sorry for myself and I've been through enough to cry myself a river and an ocean. I just want to get to know you behind the mask you wear every day. I'll be honest with you, Shayla; I still don't understand why all of these things happened to me. I didn't deserve any of them," he said, throwing a piece of paper in the trash like he was shooting basketball. He glanced over at her. "Do you ever feel like life has dumped something on you that belongs to someone else? Someone who's done really bad things, but you mistakenly got punished for it? You wanna scream, 'HEY! YOU GOT THE WRONG GUY,' but life looks at you, lets out a hearty laugh, then rolls on to its next unsuspecting victim?"

Shayla let out a loud, deep breath. "No, I

don't feel that way," she snapped. "I deserve everything that happens to me," she said coldly, not even giving Casper a glance.

"C'mon! Really, Shayla? That's the card you're gonna play?"

"What do you want me to say, Casper? Poor little me; no one ever loved me, whaaa, whaaa, whaaa. Well, I don't feel sorry for myself. I got what I deserved. Anything bad that happened to me, I deserved it, okay? I guess you're the only goodie-two-shoes in this room," she said, twisting her lips, then going back to clipping her nails.

"Annnnkkkk! Wrong answer!" he said, unmoved by her emotionless antics. "So, what do you do when life throws disappointments, hurts, and pain at you?"

She took a deep breath, obviously

annoyed by his constant questioning.

"You take it one day at a time until the hurt feels better," he said, not giving her a chance to respond. "What about failures and defeat? What do you do when you encounter those? You overcome them one day at a time as well," he quickly answered again.

She huffed. "Are you done?"

"Nope! Not until you talk to me. The point that I'm trying to make, Shayla, is when you encounter things that set you back, don't give up. Yes, it may take you a while to get back on track. No, it may not be easy, but decide where you want to go, then start heading that way. One day at a time. There's never a need to rush to get to the end. If you keep moving, you will eventually make it," Casper recommended, with his chest puffed out like he had just said something profound.

"Brav-o!" she responded aloofly.

Casper paid no attention to her tart attitude. He opened his mouth to continue his speech.

"Oh, my gosh! Are you still talking? Give it a rest, why don't you?" she grumbled.

"Well, you're still sitting here, so I can only assume you're listening. So, as I was saying, before I was so rudely interrupted...although you don't know why God has allowed these terrible things to happen to you, you must trust that trouble comes to not only make you stronger, but also for you to help someone else become stronger. This is the way the world was designed to make sure we take care of each other."

"WHAT? THAT MAKES NO SENSE! JUST

SHUT UP!" she shouted, getting off of the couch to leave.

"No, wait! Hear me out," he said, gently grabbing her arm and pulling her back down onto the couch.

"Don't touch me!" she snarled.

Casper threw both of his hands up. "I'm sorry, I didn't mean to put my hands on you."

"Just don't let it happen again," she said, sitting back down.

"I'm just saying, Shayla, when you go through something bad, if you can find a way to learn and heal from it, then you can either help others avoid going through what you went through or by seeing your strength, they can find strength of their own to heal and move towards a better life. God never promised us that the world would be without complications.

Matter of fact, he warned us time and time again that this world will be full of problems, because it is full of evil people who take joy in doing evil things. If you don't believe me, look at the life of Jesus; killed by people who hated him just because. What did he do to them? Nothing!" Casper said, looking Shayla directly into her eyes. "Shayla, the opportunity to do evil will always be there, and each person must decide whether they want to take the path of evil or of good. If they decide to take the path of evil, then they should seek to know why they're choosing that path. Most of the time, it's because someone else chose that path and they were the victim of that other person's choice. It is sad when a victim repeats the cycle of victimizing others. In saying all of that, my question to you is, are you willing to use your situation to help others or are you going to remain bitter and cold and make everyone pay for the things someone else did to you?"

Shayla didn't say a word. She gazed past Casper, looking out of the window behind him. Her eyes seemed to drift into a faraway land. Then unexpectedly, she spoke.

"I'm a typical foster kid, Casper. Unwanted, unloved, used and abused," she said solemnly. "I never knew my father and my mom was a drug addict. She never said anything nice to me, ever. She never smiled at me. Never gave me a hug or a kiss; no 'I love you,' nothing! Her family wanted nothing to do with me because my dad was black. They would call me a nigger baby. For the longest, I thought that was my nickname until I said it to a black girl at school one day and she almost knocked my head off. I never fit in anywhere. I was never white enough. I was never black enough. I was just never enough for anyone to want me or to love me. Eventually I learned to hustle to get what I want."

"What do you mean by that?"

"I did whatever it took to survive, Casper."

"Whatever it took?"

"YEAH! Whatever, and I have a stack of money in the bank to show for it."

Casper took a deep breath. He didn't know what to say, yet, he was unable to take his eyes off of this beautiful piece of artwork framed in deep wounds of disgrace and unworthiness.

"How old are you?" he asked.

"Twenty, why?"

"Twenty? Why do you still live here?"

Shayla looked away like she was ashamed

to answer.

"Do you wanna play poker?" she asked, trying to change the subject.

"Sure, but I still want to know why you're living here at twenty."

"Who are you, my father?"

"No, I'm just trying to understand you, that's all."

"Liar! You don't want to understand me! And stop being so nice, I don't like it! I don't deserve your kindness or your sympathy, so take it somewhere else!" she said, shuffling the deck of cards.

"Shayla, you had a terrible childhood and as a result, you've made terrible decisions, but that doesn't mean you're a bad person. Look at you now; raised by two parents who are perfect."

"They didn't raise me, I just told you I

raised myself. Besides, I've only known them for

two years and they are far from perfect."

"Oh! I thought—"

"Yeah, I know what you thought, but no, I

didn't live with them growing up and thank God

for that!"

"What is your problem? They've taken you

into their home and even let you stay past the

age of eighteen. There must be something

wonderful about you for them to do that."

She shrugged her shoulders

unappreciatively, and let out a 'hmph' sound.

"What does that mean?"

"Just drop it, okay?" she said, laying five

cards in front of Casper. "Stop trying to help

me. There are some people you just can't save,

Casper."

"Not true! Everyone has good and bad in

them, Shayla. It's just that you've allowed your bad to overtake your good. If you don't like what you see when you look in the mirror, you can always change it, ya know?"

She rubbed her hands on her legs like she was nervous.

"I don't even know how to begin to do that," she mumbled.

"If you want to change, then stop making excuses and come up with a plan to change."

"It's not that easy!" she growled.

"It is that easy. You said you have a lot of money in the bank, right?"

"Yeah, and don't ask for any, because I—"

"I don't want your money, Shayla, but let me ask you a question. If you could do anything you wanted to do, what would it be?"

"Anything?" she asked like a little school

girl. Then she let out a faint laugh like she was thinking of a childhood dream long forgotten.

"Yeah, anything."

She gave another uneasy laugh.

"I would be a Chef."

"A Chef? Really?"

"Not just any Chef, a Vegetarian Chef. I would go to Culinary Arts School and eventually have my own business, serving the freshest and the finest veggie dishes ever known to man."

Casper smiled.

"Good for you! I didn't know you were a Vegetarian."

"I'm not, but I would love to be one. I only eat meat because Mr. Stevens likes it. But if I had my way, the world would be a meatless society."

"Whoa, now! Let's not get carried away,"

Casper said laughing. "I love my pigs and cows."

Shayla laughed out loud. That was the first time Casper had seen Shayla laugh.

"I've never shared my dreams with anyone," she confessed.

"Why?" he asked surprisingly.

She shrugged her shoulders.

"No one has ever asked me what I wanted to do with my life before. Thank you!" she said, tapping Casper on his leg.

He could tell that something came alive inside of Shayla when she talked about her dreams. For a minute, she actually felt like she could be a Chef.

"Why won't you come up with a plan to go back to school and get your degree, then open that restaurant? You know, the only person stopping you from being a Chef is you, right?"

Casper said, picking up the cards she laid in front of him.

"I can't do that, Casper. I can't just up and leave. Mr. Stevens would not like that."

"He's not your father, Shayla. Besides, you are twenty years old. How long are you planning to stay with them? Forever?"

Shayla had never thought about life outside of the Stevens' home, and to think about it now was downright frightening.

"It's your turn," she said, throwing her cards on the table.

"Okay, I can take a hint. I'll leave it alone, but you should start thinking about your own life," he said, throwing out an Ace, King, Queen, Jack and a Ten!

"That's a Royal Flush! How did you get that?"

"Ummm, you gave it to me, remember?"

"I can't believe you got those cards! You must have cheated!" Shayla said excitedly. Then she gave Casper a weird glance. "Well, fair is fair," she said, taking off her blouse.

"What are you doing?" he asked.

"You won fair and square, didn't you?"

"Yeah, but nobody said this was Strip Poker. Shayla, you don't have to get naked to—"

Then Casper decided to just shut up and enjoy the show, because the one game he knew how to play was Poker.

With each hand they played, Shayla removed a portion of her clothes. By Casper's fourth win, there was nothing left for Shayla to remove. Then he won again. Shayla smiled, got up, and sat on his lap.

"Well, congratulations, handsome! Since I

don't have anything else to remove, I guess you'll have to start taking off some of your clothes on my behalf."

He looked down at her long naked body and brushed her hair out of her face.

"I guess I will," he responded.

Shayla wrapped her arms around him and kissed him. For some reason, this seemed like déjà vu for Casper. All he could think of was his birthday encounter with Maria. Oh, how he missed Maria. The only difference was this time he knew how to kiss. He didn't slobber on Shayla once.

Maria would be so proud of me, he thought, chuckling.

Shayla looked at him.

"What are you laughing about?"

"I'm sorry. It was nothing," he said, then

he kissed her again, trying to take his mind off of Maria.

Just as he had gotten himself focused, Mr. and Mrs. Stevens walked through the door and saw Shayla sitting on his lap naked, with her tongue as far down his throat as she could possibly get it.

Casper jumped up and pushed Shayla behind him to shield her body. He and Shayla both looked terrified, but since Shayla was the only one naked, not only did she look terrified, she also looked mortified.

Mr. Stevens looked over at the card game and became enraged.

"I THOUGHT THIS WAS OUR GAME! WHY WOULD YOU DO THIS?" he yelled, hitting the table furiously.

Casper's eyes and mouth flung open.

There was so much wrong with Mr. Stevens' reaction that Casper couldn't even begin to process it all.

Shayla looked down at the floor, shrugging her shoulders like she had no justification for her actions.

"We were just kidding around; nothing was really going to happen," she replied apologetically. "Come on, let's go," she said consolingly, reaching her hand out towards Mr. Stevens.

He gave Casper a look like he wanted to kill him, but Shayla grabbed his hand. "Come on," she said again, and like a lost puppy, he willingly followed her up the staircase.

Chapter 13

Casper stood there dumbfounded, with his eyes as wide as tennis balls while Mrs. Stevens walked into the kitchen to prepare dinner like nothing bizarre had just happened.

"What is going on, here?" Casper asked, as he ran into the kitchen behind Mrs. Stevens.

She tried to shoo him away with her hands in hopes that he would not press the issue, but that would surely not be the case.

"Mrs. Katherine, I want an answer!" he ordered, but she peacefully continued her dinner preparations as if no one was in the kitchen but her.

Unmoved by the knife she was using to cut the food, Casper placed himself in front of her and looked her straight in the eyes.

"I want to know what is going on between those two and I'm not going to stop asking until you tell me," he said.

She placed the knife on the counter and looked up at the ceiling.

"Why are you doing this?" she asked in an unbearable tone.

"No! The real question is why are you allowing this to happen?" he retorted.

"He has needs, Casper and she fulfills them for him. What do you want me to do?"

"ARE YOU SERIOUS?" he yelled.

"Yes! She wants to be with him and he wants to be with her; it's not like she's a minor or anything."

"I can't believe what I'm hearing. Another woman is upstairs having sex with your husband right now and you're telling me that you're okay with it?"

"You don't understand. Just leave it alone."

"No! I do not understand, but I am hoping you will explain it to me. I thought foster parents are supposed to help heal broken kids, not hurt them even more."

"Now, wait just a minute! No one has hurt that child! She gets whatever she wants; he loves her way more than he loves me, so don't tell me she's being hurt!"

"This is sick!"

"Don't judge us, Casper. You don't know our situation."

"Y'all are not good foster parents and I'm turning you in."

"Now listen here! We are excellent foster parents! We've been raising other folks' children since we were in our twenties and all of our foster kids have gone on and done great things with their lives. They still call us and send us gifts for our birthdays and for Christmas, so don't tell me that we've done a bad job. We loved all of our kids and would never do anything to hurt them, ever! We made those kids' lives better, not worse. We tried to do the same thing for Shayla, but—" she said, stopping abruptly in mid-sentence.

"But what? What made Shayla so unlovable?" Casper inquired with an attitude.

"You don't know her, Casper! You don't know what she's capable of."

Casper looked at Mrs. Stevens as tears rolled down her face.

"Then tell me so I can understand."

Mrs. Stevens paused, then said, "Shayla came to live with us right before she graduated high school just like you and she was after my husband and his money from the first moment she got here. She walked around the house with see-through clothes on, trying to be seductive. She would offer to rub his back when I would go grocery shopping. He would say to me, 'That girl ain't nothing but trouble; you need to send her back to where she came from,' but I always took up for her, saying, 'You know she didn't have a good upbringing, so just give her a chance.' I was the one who requested that she come live with us, so I wanted to help her. I felt I at least owed it to her to see her through high school."

Mrs. Stevens looked away like her mind had wandered off. She looked back at Casper and smiled.

"Can you believe at one time he only had eyes for me?" she said letting out a small giggle. "He would have given me the world if I asked for it; the same way he's giving her the world now," she muttered, shaking her head and wiping away tears. "He really is a good man, Casper; well, he was a good man."

"So, what happened?" Casper asked like he was still confused.

"About a week before Shayla graduated, I became very ill; very, very ill. The doctor I was going to didn't know what was wrong with me and they didn't know how to fix it. I really thought I was going to die, and so did my husband. He was worried sick about me. He retired from his job just to stay at home and take care of me. After Shayla graduated, she offered to stay and help with cooking and cleaning until I got better. I knew my husband couldn't do everything. I could tell it was already wearing him down and it had only been two weeks. I felt like I needed her, and just as she promised, she was there to take care of me. Every day, she fed me, clothed me, and made sure I had baths. She was good to me and I was very appreciative. Then one night, my husband was in the laundry room ironing his pants for the next day. She walked in there, naked as a jay bird, just like she was today. I know she was naked because I heard him ask 'Young lady, why don't you have on any clothes?' I tried to yell and tell her to leave my husband alone, but my voice was too weak. I tried to get out of bed, but

I couldn't move. I heard him say, 'Shayla, I can't do this to my wife.' I could tell she was getting to him because his voice didn't sound as strong as before. He asked her where I was and she said I was asleep. Again, he said, 'I can't do this to Katherine,' but I knew he wouldn't be able to resist her much longer. He told her how he'd never cheated on me before and how he wouldn't be able to live with himself if he did, but that was the last thing I heard before they began having sex, right on the laundry room floor. I laid in my bed and listened to the whole thing. When it was over, he couldn't even look at me. He came into our bedroom, got his night shorts, then went and slept on the couch. A few minutes later, she came in, tucked the covers in around me and left like nothing ever happened. She tried to get him to come into her bed, but he wouldn't. I heard him begging the Lord for forgiveness and promising to never let it happen again, but it did. Night after night, while I lay there dying, they had sex. I knew I couldn't do any of that for him. I figured it would only be temporary until I could get back on my feet, but I wasn't getting any better. Matter of fact, I seemed to be getting worse, but I refused to just lay there and die. One day I said to him, 'Take me to see another doctor! The one Shayla referred to me is a good friend of hers and I don't trust either one of them anymore!' He didn't ask any questions. He just put me in the car and took me to a doctor downtown. They immediately put me in the hospital, never really explaining what was wrong, but after a week or so, I was strong enough to go home. When I returned to my house, my husband was gone. I mean, he was still there physically, but emotionally, he no longer belonged to me. He never even touched me after that. He always said he didn't want to hurt me or cause any infections in my sick body. I told him I was no longer sick, but it didn't matter. Night after night, I watched him sneak out of our bedroom and into hers. I listened to them make love. Soon they stopped trying to hide it, freely having sex when and wherever they wanted. Sometimes in my bed while I was downstairs and sometimes in hers. One day, I even caught them on the living room couch. They didn't even care that I was standing there. He knew I wasn't going to leave him and she knew he wasn't going to let me put her out of the house. I didn't know what to do; I felt so helpless, so each night I just cuddled myself in my pillows and cried myself to sleep, pretending not to hear the sounds of what was once me enjoying my husband's love. I know she's only using him for his money, but he thinks she really loves him. She wouldn't know love if it beat her over the head."

"WOW," said Casper. "So, why are you putting up with this? You are a beautiful woman inside and out. You don't have to live like this. You don't have to feel trapped and helpless!" Casper said sympathetically.

"Yes, I do!" she responded. "I don't know any other life. He's the only man I've ever loved. He takes care of me and I don't have to want for anything. I don't know how to make it without him."

"This is crazy! I'm sorry, Mrs. Katherine, but I've got to get out of here."

"Wait! Please don't leave me here with them. Please, Casper. I can't take it anymore," she said, grasping onto Casper's shirt.

"Just file for divorce," Casper said, pulling away.

"Divorce? Oh, no! I can't do that. He would be so upset with me if I divorced him."

Casper looked at her like she was crazy.

"Then stay and continue putting up with this stupidity. Either way, I'm leaving."

"Wait! Wait! If you take me to see a divorce lawyer, I will give you some money to help you until you can be placed in another home."

"I'm not going to any more homes, but I will definitely take you up on that money offer."

"So you'll help me find a divorce lawyer? You know I will not be able to leave on my own."

"So, exactly how long has this been going on?" he asked.

"Two and a half years and I can't take another day of it. I feel so trapped!"

"You're only as trapped as you believe you are, Mrs. Katherine."

"Please help me!"

"Okay, okay! I'll help."

"So what will I tell Ms. Holiday when she comes by to check on you?"

"Tell her I ran away and you don't have a clue where I went."

"Will you be okay?"

"Anywhere I go will be better than where I've been, I assure you of that," he said.

"God sent you here to give me the strength to leave. I know he did. I couldn't tell anybody what was going on because I was so ashamed. Our other foster kids won't even come visit us anymore because of her."

"Shayla is a wounded girl; she needs a lot of help. She just wants to be loved like everybody else. She's really hurting, ya know?"

"I'M HURTING!" Mrs. Stevens yelled, having no regard for Shayla's past. "So, are you gonna help me or not?" she asked harshly.

"I said I'll help you, but where are you going to live?"

"I'm going to call my sister and see if I can live with her until I can find a place of my own."

"YOU'RE GONNA DO WHAT?" Mr. Stevens yelled, as he came downstairs with Shayla.

"You heard me, I'm leaving! You can have her. I hope y'all live happily ever after."

"Casper, are you leaving, too?" Shayla

asked disappointedly.

"Yeah, I can't be a part of this craziness, Shayla. What you're doing is wrong and you know it."

"Yes! I know it is, but please don't go. I'll change. I promise," she pleaded.

Mr. Stevens gave her a dirty look.

"Don't change for me, Shayla. You have to change for yourself, but if it's any consolation to you, I don't think you're as evil as you think you are. One day, I hope you find the strength to start going down a better path, then go make all of those dreams of yours come true, okay?"

Shayla smiled. "Okay," she replied.

"What dreams?" Mr. Stevens asked.

"Nothing you'd be interested in," she responded with an attitude. The she looked up at Mr. Stevens. "I'm leaving too," she said abruptly.

"WHAT? THIS IS ALL YOUR FAULT!" Mr.

Stevens shouted to Casper. "What have you told

them?" he asked, walking towards Casper like

he was ready to fight. "Get out of my house and

don't you ever come back," he ordered.

"Gladly," Casper replied, not even

bothering to pack any of his things. He just

grabbed his jacket and headed towards the door.

"Wait! I still need that lawyer," Mrs.

Stevens said, quickly trotting behind Casper

with keys to their paid off Jaguar in her hand.

They headed outside and she unlocked the

car door for Casper to get in.

"What do you think you're doing?" Mr.

Stevens yelled like he was distraught. "Are you

really going to throw away thirty-eight years of

marriage, Katherine?"

Mrs. Stevens didn't say a word. She had gotten a glimpse of freedom and there was nothing left in her past that she wanted in her future.

"I know you hear me, Katherine! KATHERINE!" Mr. Stevens yelled.

Casper looked back at Shayla. She and Mr. Stevens were both standing in the doorway looking sad and destitute.

Casper rolled down his window and smiled at Shayla. "I like my veggie burgers with pepper jack cheese and blue cheese dressing, on them, okay? Make sure it's on the menu," he shouted out.

She gave him a big smile.

"I will! I'll name it the Casper Burger," she shouted back, as Casper and Mrs. Stevens backed out of the driveway.

"What is that fool talking about?" Mr.

Stevens asked as Shayla made a phone call and

asked someone to come pick her up.

"Who are you calling and where do you

think you're going?" he asked, but she politely

ignored him.

"I'll be walking down the highway, so

please hurry!" she said to the person on the

phone.

"Shayla, I asked you a question. Where do

you think you're going?" he inquired again.

"I'm going to be somebody," she said

proudly, as she hung up the phone, walked out

of the door, and headed towards her new

beginning.

Chapter 14

"Look! That sign says Attorney at Law," Casper pointed out, beckoning Mrs. Stevens to turn into the parking lot of a tall brick building.

"Oh, thank goodness!" she said, eagerly pulling into the parking lot and parking the car. She leaned back in her seat and folded her arms. "Well, here I am," she whispered.

"Are you sure you're ready to do this?" Casper asked.

"I need to do this! My husband is not the same man I married. The man I fell in love with would never hurt me the way this man has. Too much damage has been done and I don't even want to repair it anymore."

"I understand, but some relationships have endured greater challenges than yours and couples still managed to make things work."

"Are you telling me to go back to that unfaithful—"

"Noooo! No! I would never tell you to do that, but let me ask this, do the two horrible years that you just endured outweigh the thirty-six wonderful years he has given you?"

"Why are you asking me that? I thought you wanted me to divorce him."

"No, I wanted you to stop putting up with his infidelity and disrespect, but I never said divorce was the only way to accomplish that goal. We're talking thirty-eight years here, Mrs. Katherine; that's a long time and ninety-eight percent of it was beautiful. I just don't want you to make a rash decision and then have regrets."

"But, you saw how he—"

"Let me ask you another question," Casper interrupted. "If Shayla was no longer in the picture and he vowed to never cheat on you again, would you take him back?"

She stared out of the window with a muddled look on her face.

"Well, I don't know. He's hurt me so bad, Casper. I just don't—"

"If he promised to never, ever do that to you again, would you want him back?"

"Well, I guess I would."

"Then you're not ready to file for divorce. When you're really ready for a relationship to be over, it doesn't matter what the other person promises, nothing will make you go back to them. If there is any part of you that still wants the relationship to work, then divorce is not your

answer. Be true to yourself, Mrs. Katherine,

even if you feel like you're being a fool."

"Then what should I do?" Mrs. Stevens

asked, sounding like she was totally confused.

Casper smiled.

"In my opinion, you should still go live

with your sister for a few weeks or maybe even a

few months just to clear your head. If he comes

back and asks for a second chance, then you

can suggest the two of you go to marriage

counseling. If he agrees and everything goes

well, maybe you can start dating again. If he

woos you to your liking, then perhaps he could

ask for your hand in remarriage," Casper said

smiling. "Who knows, maybe you guys can put

the past totally behind you and live happily ever

after."

Mrs. Stevens gave Casper a big grin, then her face dropped.

"I would love to date my husband again, but he's in love with someone else, now."

"No, he is infatuated with someone else now. That is not love. How about we say he just lost his mind for two years. I think you leaving him will help him find it, though," Casper said smiling.

"You think so?"

"Did you see how horrified he looked when you told him you were leaving?"

Mrs. Stevens laughed.

"He did look pretty torn apart, didn't he?"

"Yes he did," Casper agreed. "Sometimes separations are good. It helps people to see what their life would be like without the other person in it and it also helps them appreciate all

the little things they took for granted. How
about you try the separation thing first and if he
still doesn't change, then at least you know
where the divorce lawyer's office is," he said,
chuckling.

"That sounds like a great plan, Casper.
Thank you so much, but I think I'll still go inside
the building and pick up a business card, just in
case," she said smiling.

"Yes, that may be a good idea," Casper
replied. "Well, I think my work here is done," he
joked.

Casper gave Mrs. Stevens a hug, but just
as he was about to get out of the car, her phone
rang.

"Hello," she answered, motioning Casper
to not leave yet.

"Hi, Mrs. Stevens, this is Joan Holiday,

the social worker from—"

"Oh, hi, Ms. Holiday. What can I do for you?" she asked, elbowing Casper in his arm.

Casper sat there with an, *I don't care who's on the phone, I'm not going to any more homes,* look on his face.

"I was just calling to check on you guys. Is everything okay?"

"Yeah, sure. Why would you ask that?"

"Well, Mr. Stevens called and he sounded pretty upset. He said you left him and you took Casper with you and he didn't think either of you were coming back."

Casper rolled his eyes, as he overheard the conversation, but Mrs. Stevens giggled as if she was very happy that her husband would send the social worker to track her down.

"That silly man! He is a mess," she said

laughing. "I have not left him, we just had a little spat, that's all."

"And what about Casper? He said you were going to help him leave. Mrs. Stevens, you know Casper is still a minor and he belongs to this institution. Assisting a minor in running away is against the law. You understand that, correct?"

Mrs. Stevens and Casper gave each other a long stare while Ms. Holiday waited patiently for a response.

"Ms. Holiday, I have no idea what you are talking about. I dropped Casper off at the park to play basketball about twenty minutes ago. He's fine."

"Oh, okay. That's good to hear," Ms. Holiday said, sounding relieved. "I would like to stop by tomorrow to make sure everything is okay, alright?"

"Ummmm, tomorrow?"

"Yes, is there a problem?"

"Oh, no. There's no problem. Tomorrow will be fine. Casper and I will be waiting on you."

"Okay, thank you so much!"

"No! Thank you!" Mrs. Stevens said, hanging up the phone and turning to Casper.

"Casper, if you try to get a job as a runaway orphan, they are going to find you and take you back to Ms. Holiday. Maybe you should come live with me and my sister until you turn eighteen."

"NOOOO! I'm tired of going from home to home. I'm tired! I just want to be on my own," he said. "No matter where that is, I just want to be left alone."

"Okay, I understand," Mrs. Stevens said, slightly rubbing Casper's shoulder. "Thank you for everything, Casper. I wouldn't have ever gotten the courage to do this if you hadn't come to live with us. Here's some money to help you get on your feet," she said, handing him a wad of twenty dollar bills. "There's a bus station across the street," she pointed. "Get you a ticket and go somewhere nice, okay?"

"Okay."

"Promise me that you'll take care of yourself, young man."

"I promise, and I hope your new life is full of happiness," he said, giving her another hug.

"Oh, it will be. Now get outta here before Ms. Holiday figures out that I lied to her," she said smiling.

Casper smiled back. "Okay," he replied,

getting out of the car and walking towards the

bus station.

Chapter 15

"What can I do for you, hun?" the lady behind the ticket window asked as Casper approached the window.

"I would like a one-way ticket to Tribuckle, Tennessee, please."

"Tribuckle? Sweetie, the closest we'll get to Tribuckle is Nashville, then it's still about an hour and a half drive from there."

"An hour and a half??"

"Yes! Tribuckle is South of us! Our bus only goes North to Nashville. You'll have to get off when you get there and buy another ticket to go South to Chattanooga. Tribuckle is thirty minutes from Chattanooga, so you'll still have to get someone to come pick you up from there. Unless you decide to walk, but I wouldn't recommend that," she said laughing.

Casper didn't laugh at all. He seemed very upset.

"Why can't I just buy a ticket to Chattanooga?"

"Like I said, our bus line only goes to Nashville. When you get to Nashville, you can buy a ticket then. The Nashville bus line will take you anywhere you want to go," she said reassuringly.

Casper huffed.

"How much is a ticket to Nashville?"

"A one-way ticket will be twenty bucks, sweetheart."

Casper begrudgingly gave the lady the
money, then got onto the bus.

Casper had never been on public
transportation before. He was checking out
everything and everyone.

Uuuuuhhh, okay, he thought, looking at a
lady passing by in pink leggings and an orange
and black shirt so small that it looked like it
belonged to someone's four-year-old daughter.
What was most memorable, though was her
shiny hot pink shoes and blue hair. Casper
tried hard not to look, but he just sat there,
staring her up and down as she passed.

"What are you looking at?" she growled.

"Nothing!" Casper said quickly and turned
away.

"Oh, you're calling me nothing?" she
argued.

"No! I think you're something," he countered, offending her even more.

"So, you think that I'm something, as in something else?" she scoffed.

"Move it along, ma'am," the bus driver grumbled. "We have several people wanting to get on the bus."

She rolled her eyes at Casper, then walked to the back of the bus.

"That was a pretty close call," a gentleman whispered to Casper. "She looked like she could take you. I wasn't gonna be able to help you with that one," the guy said, letting out an overly excited laugh.

Casper smiled, then decided it might be best if he just kept his mouth shut for the rest of the ride to Nashville.

Casper snuggled next to a window and

made himself comfortable. For the first time in his life, Casper felt free and in charge.

Riding the bus isn't so bad, although, it's definitely not my preferred mode of transportation. This is a really great feeling, he thought as he closed his eyes to take a nap.

The next thing Casper heard was, "Last call for Marietta, Georgia! Last Call."

Casper jumped up! "Marietta, Georgia? I was supposed to get off the bus in Nashville," he said out loud.

"Nashville? Son, that stop was three hours ago. We're in Georgia now. I called out three times for Nashville; were you in another world or something?"

"I guess I was asleep."

"Well, it must have been a deep sleep," he said sarcastically.

"Yeah, I'm a very deep sleeper, but I thought this bus line didn't travel down South? The lady at the last bus station told me I would have to get off the bus and buy another ticket to get to Chattanooga."

"I don't know why she told you that. We change bus drivers in Nashville; maybe that's what she meant, but this is my route and I always go to Chattanooga and all parts of Georgia."

"But aren't you supposed to make sure everyone is off the bus before you start your next route?"

The guy gave Casper a defiant look. "Yes, and as far as I'm concerned, I did check the bus and NO ONE was on it. Is there anyone that would like to tell me differently?" the guy said.

Casper just shook his head.

"I'm not looking for any trouble, man. Just tell me what I need to do to get to Chattanooga."

"Buy another ticket," the guy said with an attitude.

Casper jumped off the bus and headed to the ticket window.

"A one-way ticket to Chattanooga, please."

"That'll be forty dollars, hun," the lady said in a deep Southern accent.

"Dang! The prices for these tickets just keep going up, I see," Casper said, reaching into his coat pocket.

He gave the lady a fearful look. "I know I put my money in this pocket," he said nervously. He patted the other pocket. "Where is my money?" he said.

"NEXT," she yelled as if she thought

Casper was playing some childish game.

"WAIT! I had money. Just let me find it," he said, wildly patting all over his body. "WHERE IS MY MONEY?" he screamed. "Hold on, I'll be right back," he said.

The lady twisted her lips, "I'll be here all day, sugar," she replied nonchalantly.

He ran back onto the bus.

"Hey! I need your ticket," the bus driver said.

"I left something. I need to go back and look for it."

"There's nothing on this bus. I just did a clean sweep through every seat," the guy said mockingly.

Casper looked over at him and gave him a *yeah, right* look.

"Is there someone here to say I didn't?" he

said trying to pick up where he and Casper left off.

Casper ignored him and continued to look frantically in every seat.

"What did you lose?" the guy asked.

"ALL OF MY MONEY!" Casper yelled.

"Oh, you can kiss that good-bye, son. As hard as you were sleeping, anybody could have taken your money and you wouldn't have felt a thing. Where did you have it?"

"In this pocket right here," Casper said, pointing to the right pocket on the outside of his jacket.

"Oh, good grief! Y'all kids don't know a thing about survival. You should have at least had it in the pocket next to the window. No one would have been able to reach it over there. We typically don't have any trouble on our bus lines, but if you put your money in plain view so someone can see it, you're almost begging them to steal it. Everybody doesn't have good morals," the bus driver said, like he had forgiven Casper for their earlier altercation.

"That's all the money I had. How am I going to get to Chattanooga, now?"

The bus driver stared out the window as if he didn't hear Casper.

"Well, I really just need to get to Tribuckle, Tennessee. How far is that from here?" Casper asked.

"Tribuckle is about an hour and fifteen minutes."

"Awww, man! That's too far! Can you drop me off as you're passing through the town?" Casper pleaded.

The bus driver laughed. "Oh, no, sir! I'll

lose my job if I do that. I can get you to

Chattanooga, but you still need a ticket. I can't

take you anywhere without a ticket."

"Well can you just help me get back to

Nashville where I was originally supposed to go?"

"Not without a ticket!"

"BUT YOU KNOW SOMEONE STOLE ALL

OF MY MONEY!" Casper yelled.

"Now, look! I'm trying to be nice to your

snot nose self. I suggest you calm down before I

ban you from my bus. Besides, I'm on my break

right now and I'd like to enjoy it in peace before I

have to load up for my next route."

"Your next route? What about me? I need

to get to Tribuckle."

"Son, there's nothing I can do for you."

"So, you're gonna leave me in Marietta?"

"YOU HAVE NO TICKET!"

"I HAD A TICKET!"

"GET OFF MY BUS BEFORE I CALL THE COPS!" he shouted.

The bus driver puffed out his chest like he was big and bad and Casper stared him down like he was mentally daring him to kick him off the bus. Casper came to his senses, though, because he definitely didn't want to go to jail.

Jail would not be a step up, he thought. Casper looked down at the floor like he wanted to cry. He didn't know what he was going to do if he couldn't get back to Tribuckle.

"Look, I'm sorry someone stole your money. Really, I am, but there's nothing I can do for you. Folks are starting to gather outside the bus, and I have to load up for my next route. I don't want to have you arrested, but I will if you don't exit the bus," the bus driver said peacefully.

Casper took a deep breath. He looked at all the people patiently waiting for the bus driver to announce that they could start boarding the bus. He calmly turned around, let out a growl, then quietly stepped off the bus.

He went back to the ticket window and tried to talk his way into a free ticket. He offered to sweep the floors, pick up trash, and even carry people's luggage onto the bus for them, but nothing worked and people were starting to feel harassed. Then he asked for a job application, but by that time the lady at the window had had enough and she told him to leave the building.

He went outside and laid on the bench. Words could not describe the hopelessness Casper felt. It would soon be night fall and he had no money, no food, no phone, no one's

phone number, and no idea what would happen

to him next.

Chapter 16

As each day passed, the bus station bench is where Casper found himself. Most people were nice to him, offering him food or hot chocolate. He would only eat a little at a time because he wasn't sure when would be the next time he ate. This is not the kind of freedom he imagined when he left the Stevens' but at least he was free. Besides, living at the bus station wasn't so bad. That was until someone complained.

"Why are you letting a homeless man stay at the bus station? Is this the kind of place you guys are running?" a grumpy old man said to the Security Officer.

"I'll take care of it," the officer said, but the truth was, he felt sorry for Casper and no one really viewed him as homeless. They just thought of him as the guy who got robbed on the bus; he wasn't hurting anyone.

"Hey," the Security Officer said, tapping Casper on his shoulder, trying to wake him up.

Casper rubbed his eyes. "Yes, sir?"

"I'm sorry, man, but you're gonna have to find somewhere else to go. People are starting to complain."

"Oh!" was all Casper said as he gathered up the few items people had given him along the way.

"Here's a backpack. You can put all of your things in here," the Security Officer said.

"Thanks," Casper responded appreciatively, as he threw his things in the backpack and walked off, with no clue where he was going.

Casper walked and walked until it was almost nightfall. He saw a large box near some abandoned steps so he figured that could shield him for the night until daylight came. He was lying comfortably inside the box when the next thing he heard was, "WHAT ARE YOU DOING IN MY HOUSE?"

Casper jumped up and saw two big men standing over him. Before Casper could answer, one of the men grabbed him and threw him up against something hard and that's all Casper remembered.

It is unknown what actually happened to Casper that night, but when he woke up, he was in a strange place surrounded by a bunch of

homeless people.

"Where am I?" he asked a lady that was

standing over him rejoicing that he had regained

consciousness.

"He's alive!" she screamed at several other

people who were in the home.

They all came over to look at him.

Casper looked around at this place they

called home. All the windows were boarded up

and they had several candles lit for lighting.

The people who were standing around

Casper were beyond scary. They looked like

they hadn't bathed in months, maybe even

years, and the place they were in smelled like a

cross between a chicken farm, pig slop, cow

manure, and freshly baked apple pies from two

years ago.

Oh, my gosh, Casper thought, trying to keep from vomiting. He leaned forward, trying to get up, but he was overcome with pain.

"AAAAHHHHH!" he screamed, "Why does my body hurt all over?"

"Ummm, you were left for dead in the alley, man. I don't know what you were thinking. Trying to steal Roscoe's house is just like asking for a death sentence," said one man.

"Who is Roscoe? And I didn't try to steal anyone's house."

"Roscoe and his brother, Andy own the abandoned box that sits on the porch, dum-dum! Everybody knows that!"

"Except him," one man joked, pointing to Casper.

"Roscoe disappears for a few days each month, but when he returns, his house better be the same way he left it. When he got back this time, you were in it asleep!" a guy said, chuckling.

"I can't believe you did that," another man said, shaking his head and walking off. The rest of the guys all started laughing.

"God must be shining down on you," the lady mentioned, "because you should be dead right now."

"That's for sure," someone else chimed in. "After we heard that Roscoe dumped your body in the alley, we went there to find you. We all thought you were dead. We were going to at least give you a proper burial, but Louise said you still had a pulse. She used to be the Head Nurse at the hospital downtown, ya know?"

Casper looked over at the woman who was still standing over him smiling; he assumed she must be Louise. Casper smiled back.

"I don't know if you'll ever walk again, but I was able to wrap up your broken leg and we have some crutches that we found in the dumpster a few months ago that you can have."

"Louise said those crutches would come in handy," someone mentioned.

Casper looked deep into this woman's eyes. She kinda reminded him of his grandma. She had long stringy grey hair that she kept pulled back into a ponytail. She had very dark circles under her eyes. It looked like she'd been through a lot in life. He wanted to ask her how she became homeless after being a Head Nurse for a major hospital, but he didn't want to upset her.

"I also worked with physical therapy patients," Louise said to Casper.

Casper gave her a strange look.

"Maybe I can help you walk again, if the damage isn't too bad. Right now, it's too soon to tell."

"Oh! Okay. Thank you! I appreciate all your help."

"You're definitely a trouper," she said, patting Casper on the shoulder.

"So I've been told," he responded.

"God definitely has a plan for you, young man. He has a plan for all of us, even if we're homeless," Louise said, walking away.

"Louise!" Casper called out.

"Yes," she said, turning back around.

"Thank you!"

"No! Thank God," she said, then walked out the front door.

A few months later, Casper was back up

and walking on his own, although he was left with a slight limp. Everyone, including Louise, still said it was a miracle.

One day Casper and some of his homeless friends were downtown trying to collect money to buy groceries, which was their weekly routine.

While walking, they saw a pregnant lady and her husband walking towards them.

"Hi, sir and ma'am, we're trying to buy some groceries. Do you have any money you can give us?" one guy said.

"We don't have any cash on us at the moment," the gentleman responded, "But tomorrow is Friends and Family Day at our church. You should come out and celebrate with us. Maybe I'll have something to give you then."

"Man! We're just asking you for some

money, not all that church stuff," he replied.

"What time does service start?" one of the other guys asked, feeling desperate for some sort of hope to his life.

"It starts at 10:00 a.m.," the lady said smiling.

"I'll be there," the guy said.

"Good! We look forward to seeing you," the lady and gentleman said simultaneously, then turned to walk away.

"And congratulations on your baby," one homeless guy said.

She looked back as she and her husband were walking in the other direction. "Thank you, it's our first," she said, excitedly.

The couple kept walking, and eventually disappeared into the distance. The entire homeless gang stared at them as they walked away. For one miniscule moment, they all

wondered if one day they would ever experience

that kind of love and happiness.

Chapter 17

On Sunday morning, when the pregnant lady and her husband arrived at church, three of the homeless guys were patiently waiting outside on a bench.

"Hey, guys!" they said to them as they walked up the steps. "We're glad you came! Come on in."

"Nah, I think I'll just stay out here and listen to the service," one of the guys said.

"Yeah, we don't want to offend anyone," another one chimed in.

"Offend anyone?" the lady disputed. "God

loves everybody, and everybody includes you."

The guys all looked at her like the love
that she was speaking of didn't apply to them.

"Guys you really are welcome to come in.
That's why we invited you," her husband chimed
in.

One of the guys got up and walked in
behind them, but the other two stayed outside.

"That's a shame that your friends feel they
can't come into a church," she said.

"They just don't want to hinder the
service, that's all," the guy said.

She shook her head in disappointment.

"You can sit wherever you want," her
husband said to him.

The guy found himself a comfortable spot
on the back row. He picked up a Bible and
began reading it while he waited for the service

to start. He was unsure how the Bible landed on this particular scripture, but he had no doubt that it was meant for him. It said, "We have trouble all around us, but we are not defeated. We often don't know what to do, but we do not give up. We are mistreated, but God will never leave us. We are hurt sometimes, but we will not be destroyed."

As the homeless guy read this scripture, he began thinking about all that he'd been through and how he somehow overcame all of it. He began to cry. He tried to stop the tears, but they could not be stopped. He got several weird stares, but a lady who had just sat in front of him turned around and gave him some tissue.

"It's going to work out," she said to him.

"Thank you," he said, wiping his tears and trying to gather his composure.

A few minutes before church started, two other ladies walked in and sat beside the lady in front of the homeless guy like they knew her.

"Uuugghh, he stinks," one of the ladies whispered.

"Michelle, don't say that," the lady sitting there said scoldingly.

"Girl, you know I'm not lying. Saidah, am I lying?" she asked the other lady that came in with her, but she kept looking forward like she wanted nothing to do with someone insulting a homeless person at church.

"What took y'all so long to come in? I've been sitting here for at least ten minutes by myself," the lady said.

"Saidah had to put on her makeup. You know how long—"

"Look! There's Kirsten," the other lady

yelled, cutting Michelle off in mid-sentence.

The pregnant lady came running over, giving all of them hugs like she hadn't seen them in years.

"I'm so glad you guys could come," she said. "I miss you so much."

"O.M.G! Kirsten, I can't believe how fat you are!" Michelle blurted out.

"Don't you mean how fine I am?"

"No, I said what I meant," Michelle responded with a small chuckle, rubbing the pregnant lady's stomach.

"What-ever! Hey Saidah! Hey Beatriz! You guys look amazing. I'm so glad to see you," she said, giving them another hug.

"Hi, did they say your name was Kirsten?" the homeless guy asked, interrupting their happy moment.

"I'm sorry I didn't introduce myself. Yes, my name is Kirsten and my husband's name is Everett. These are—"

"I'm sorry for disturbing you and your friends, but I really gotta go to the restroom. Can you tell me where it is?" he asked, sounding like he had waited as long as he could.

Michelle and Saidah gave Kirsten a weird look.

Kirsten smiled. "You guys, this is Everett's and my special guest for today. His name is—wait, what is your name?"

Just then someone called Kirsten up to welcome everyone to the church's annual Family and Friends Day.

"I'm sorry, I have to go. The restroom is in the foyer to your right," Kirsten said, hurrying to the front of the church and giving a hearty welcome to everyone that came.

"See, Michelle!" the lady named Beatriz said. "That homeless guy was invited to church by Kirsten and Everett! You need to be careful how you treat people; he could actually be an angel in disguise, ya know?"

Michelle looked embarrassed.

"I'm sorry, Lord," she whispered, then all the girls joined in with the choir and sang. The homeless guy eventually returned back to his seat and joined in with them.

♫ ♪ ♫ *Here I am to worship* ♫ ♪ ♫ *Here I am to bow down. Here I am to say that you're my God.* ♫ ♪ ♫

After the praise and worship portion of the service was over, Michelle felt so bad for how she acted towards him, she went over and placed a twenty dollar bill in his hand.

"Oh, thank you! Thank you!" he said graciously.

It was a very good thing Michelle had asked for forgiveness and made amends with the homeless guy, because the pastor's sermon was about loving those who don't look or act like you.

"Maybe there's a small chance that you'll still make it into heaven," Saidah whispered to Michelle, then let out a small giggle.

After church, Kirsten and Everett walked up to the homeless guy, gave him twenty-five dollars and told him to come back to visit whenever he wanted.

Saidah nudged Beatriz.

"They just gave him money too! This guy is making out like a bandit today, isn't he?" she whispered.

Kirsten and Everett went over to the three ladies and they all gave Everett big hugs.

"Everett, I swear you looker finer every time I see you," said Beatriz, deciding not to respond to what Saidah just said about the money the homeless guy was given.

"I love you like a sister, Beatriz, but I will cut you over this one," Kirsten replied.

Everett couldn't help but blush, showing off his beautiful deep dimples.

"She's right though, Kirsten. Your man is fine. Look at those dimples," Michelle chimed in.

Kirsten gave dirty looks to both Beatriz and Michelle.

"I appreciate the compliments, ladies, but please stop," Everett requested. "If you upset Kirsten, she's going to cancel the trip y'all have planned for next week and she'll have to stay at home with me. You know that would totally ruin my Monday night football party that I have planned with the guys! I'll lose my man-card if I have my wife there! Do you want that to happen?" asked Everett with a serious look on his face. "Not that I don't want you around," he clarified, giving Kirsten a quick kiss on the cheek.

"Yeah, yeah! Whatever! I'm not gonna ruin your Monday night male bonding party. Is Daniel coming?" Kirsten asked Everett.

"Yeah, he and Melah are out of town, but they should be back sometime tomorrow morning."

"Who the heck is Daniel?" Michelle inquired.

"He's my neighbor from back home. He

and his wife, Melah moved up here last year. She's going to meet us in Tennessee. Is that okay with everyone?" Kirsten asked her friends.

"Sure," said Beatriz.

"Fine with me," said Saidah.

"Ummm, No!" said Michelle. "We don't know her like that. Why do we need to bring someone else into the group?"

Saidah shook her head.

"So much for you making it into heaven," Saidah said to Michelle.

Everett, Kirsten, and Beatriz just looked at Michelle in disbelief.

"Shelly, are you jealous?" Kirsten asked.

"Yup!" Saidah answered before Michelle could get the words out.

"No, I'm not jealous. I just don't know her, that's all. It's always been the four of us. I just don't see why we need to bring in a fifth wheel."

Everett gave Michelle a blank stare.

"Okay, Kirsten, I'll be in the car," he said, walking off.

"Go on home, baby. I'll catch a ride with the girls."

"Okay, I'll see you all later."

"Bye Everett," all the ladies said at the same time.

"Y'all better stay away from my husband," Kirsten barked.

"Nobody wants your husband, girl, with his cute self," Saidah replied.

"Come on, let's go," Michelle said, then they all jumped in the car and headed to Kirsten's house.

Chapter 18

When the ladies got to Kirsten's house, they hurried and ate lunch, then excitedly gathered their things for their girls' trip to Tennessee.

"Bye," Everett said as they ran out of the front door like they were teenagers going to a wild party. "Honey, please be careful in your condition, okay? You know you're not as light on your feet as you used to be."

All the girls stared at Everett with evil eyes.

"And all this time, we thought you were

perfect and above saying stupid things," Michelle said to Everett.

"Was I not supposed to say that?" he asked nervously.

"NO!" they all yelled, as Kirsten threw a bottle of water at him.

"Thanks, baby. How did you know I was thirsty?" he asked, coming towards the car to give Kirsten a kiss goodbye, but Michelle put the car in drive and spun off, leaving him standing there with his lips puckered in the air.

"Love you too, babe," he yelled, laughing as they drove off.

It was obvious that the girls had a lot to catch up on because they talked all the way to Tennessee. Michelle put the address to where they were going in the GPS, but when it said, "You have reached your destination," they were in front of a campground. They all looked at Beatriz like they were confused.

"I think the GPS took us to the wrong place, Beatriz. What is the address again?" Michelle asked.

"What? This is the right place," she said, jumping out of the car and pulling the tent off of the top of Michelle's truck.

"What is this place?" Saidah asked.

"It doesn't matter, because I'm not staying here," Michelle said.

"It's a campground. I told y'all we were going camping," Beatriz explained.

"We didn't think you actually meant outside in a tent, though," Kirsten added.

"So, where exactly do you go camping?" Beatriz asked sarcastically.

"IN A HOTEL!" they all said.

"Michelle and Saidah, you saw me put this tent on the top of the truck. What exactly did you think it was for?" Beatriz asked sternly.

"Ummm, we didn't know why you put that thing up there, but we surely didn't think you were crazy enough to try and take us camping," said Michelle.

Beatriz looked over at Saidah, who was nodding her head in agreement with Michelle.

"Y'all are unbelievable!" Beatriz said. "You asked me to plan our next trip, so I did. I planned the whole thing and you don't even appreciate it," she said, pushing the tent back on the top of the truck.

"Wait, Beatriz! We're sorry," said Kristen.

"Me too," Saidah chimed in. "We'll give it a try, okay?"

"No! We will not give it a try," Michelle

countered. "We can get a hotel and come back to this place tomorrow, during the daylight, but I'm not sleeping out here with bears and wolves and spiders and snakes. No thank you!" she fused, then looked at Beatriz and said, "Sweetie, tomorrow we will do whatever you want, but we're going to a hotel tonight, okay?"

Beatriz huffed and gave Michelle a judgmental look.

"Don't look at me like that; you've known us since the third grade. You knew good and doggone well we were not going to stay outside at a campground. You should have reserved a hotel, but since you didn't, I will go do that right now."

"Wait!" Saidah called out to Michelle.

Michelle turned around to see what Saidah wanted.

Saidah gave Michelle a serious look,
"First," she said, "Don't ever let me hear you say
'good and doggone well' again, and second, let's
at least give this camping thing a try, since
Beatriz put so much effort into planning it."

"I'm in," Kirsten agreed.

They all looked over at Michelle.

"I'm not in," Michelle said.

"Come on, Michelle?" Beatriz pleaded.

"Okay, okay! I'll stay out here for two
hours, then I'm leaving," Michelle grumbled.

"Great!" Beatriz said excitedly, grabbing
the tent and pulling it back off of Michelle's
truck. All the girls gathered around to help her.

Beatriz was in Girl Scouts for most of her
childhood, so she knew all about camping. The
other ladies knew nothing, so they happily let
Beatriz lead the way.

"Go get some twigs so we can build a fire," Beatriz shouted eagerly.

"Twigs? No one says twigs," Saidah pointed out, but Beatriz was too thrilled about camping to allow anyone to ruin her mood.

After they got the tent set up and the fire going, Beatriz brought out the marshmallows and hotdogs.

"Here, grab one and put it on the end of a stick. Then gently place it over the fire," Beatriz instructed.

"I hope these hotdogs come with fries and a drink," Michelle whispered to Saidah.

"What is with you this weekend, Michelle?" Beatriz asked. "You've been so funky and judgmental since you arrived at church on Sunday."

"She's always funky and judgmental,"

Saidah stated.

"No, something is wrong. I can tell,"

Beatriz mentioned.

Michelle got quiet.

"Nothing is wrong," she insisted.

"Let me look into your eyes," Kirsten said,

grabbing Michelle's face and turning it towards

hers. Kirsten squinted and looked into

Michelle's eyes like she was examining them.

"Yeah, something's wrong. What are you

keeping from us?" Kirsten said sternly to

Michelle.

"Nothing!"

"Don't lie to me, Shelly."

"No! Really, nothing is wrong," Michelle

said pulling away from Kirsten. "Other than

finding out that my husband is cheating on me

and now having to decide if I'm going to divorce

him or just pretend nothing is going on so I can keep my family together, that's all. No biggie!" Michelle said helplessly.

"WHAT?" Beatriz and Saidah said.

"I don't believe that! Matt would never cheat on you, Shelly," Kirsten said reassuringly.

"That's what I thought too, but he keeps getting these strange phone calls and texts. Then next thing I know, he tells me he'll be right back. He thinks I don't hear a woman's voice on the other end, but I hear her. It's like he sits and waits on her to call. I don't know if he ever waited on me to call him like that, but I refuse to cry over it. If he wants to cheat then he can have her," Michelle said angrily, throwing her stick as far as she could, mistakenly dropping a hotdog on the ground.

"Hey! That was a perfectly good hotdog,"

Beatriz fussed. "Now I have to go wash it off in the lake."

"Beatriz! Really? Try being a little sensitive, why don't you!" said Saidah, as Beatriz picked the hotdog up off of the ground and hustled down to the lake to rinse it off.

Kirsten turned back to Michelle, who had just pulled out a bottle of liquor and started drinking it straight from the bottle.

"SHELLY!" Kirsten yelled. "When did you start drinking?"

"When I lost my husband," she said, taking another gulp, and putting her head down so no one would see her crying. Kirsten put her arm around Michelle and said, "Honey, you can't drink your problems away. Besides, maybe there's something else going on. Have you asked him?"

"NO! Why would I ask him?"

"Why wouldn't you ask him?" Saidah barked.

"If I ask him and he says yes, then what? I'll be forced to make a decision that I don't know that I want to make. I don't want to lose my husband, you guys. I love him more than anything."

"So, you're gonna just let him cheat?" asked Saidah.

"I have two babies at home. I don't want to be a single mother like my mom was. I know what that was like. I'm just not going to do that to my kids. I want them to have their father, even if that means turning my back on his infidelity."

"YOU'RE CRAZY!" Saidah shouted. "You and your children will be fine. That is never a good reason to stay in a marriage with an

unfaithful man. There are too many diseases

out there, Michelle. When men cheat, they get

very sloppy and careless. For one, they don't

use condoms and on top of that, they don't even

know how to keep their affairs discrete. They

are all downtown with their mistress, hugged up

as if they don't have a wife and five hundred

kids sitting at home waiting on them to come

back from the store with that jar of peanut

butter they sent him to get. The dummy stays

gone for two hours and still forgets to bring the

peanut butter home. Then he comes up with a

ridiculous lie and you're just looking at him like

'Boo Boo The Fool, at least bring back the

peanut butter, so these kids can make their

sandwich.' You finally start putting two and two

together, but everybody in town already knew he

was cheating, because they've all seen them together. No! I'm not walking around looking like a fool for nobody. He can go on with his side chick, while I file for alimony, child support, emotional damage, defamation of character, pain and suffering, and anything else I can think of. It might not get him to stay, but I promise, he'll think about me every time he sees me riding around in that Mercedes Benz that he's paying for," Saidah argued.

Kirsten chimed in. "Oh, good grief, Saidah," she said in an aggravated tone. "Does it really take all of that? If a man doesn't want you, then just let him go in peace. Why would you try to make his life miserable?"

"Because he made my life miserable! At one point he wanted me, so what he needs to do is figure out how to get back to that point. It's cheaper to keep her, honey!" Saidah replied.

Michelle just stared at Saidah, wondering if Saidah was still giving advice to her or if she had ventured off into a world of her own.

Michelle took another gulp of liquor. "It's different whenz you find yasuf in the sit-u-a-tion, Sai-dah," said Michelle, slurring her words. "Until you are going through it yasuf, you really can't say whatz you'd do," she said, taking several more sips of liquor, then sticking her tongue in the bottle, trying to get the last drop.

"Put that bottle down," Kirsten said, snatching it out of Michelle's hand.

"GET YOUR STUFF! GET YOUR STUFF! LET'S GO! LET'S GO!" Beatriz yelled, huffing as she ran back from the lake.

"Why? We were just getting comfortable," Kirsten said.

"No! We're leaving! Let's go! There's something in those bushes down there and I'm not staying to find out what it is!" Beatriz said as she was still huffing and puffing, and pouring dirt on the fire to put it out.

"Hey! That fire was keeping us warm," Saidah contended.

"I'll just stay here and die," Michelle said, flopping herself onto the ground and laying there like she had nothing to live for.

"What is wrong with her?" Beatriz asked.

"Nothing!" Saidah said, throwing hotdogs at Michelle, who was still lying on the ground.

Michelle didn't complain. She just picked up one of the hotdogs that had landed on her shirt and ate it.

"Oh, my gosh!" Beatriz said. "I don't know what is going on with y'all, but I sure hope it's fixed by the time I get back. I'm going to go call around and try to get us a hotel."

"Stay close so we can see you," said Kirsten.

"I'm just going over here by this tree," Beatriz responded.

"Michelle, give me your phone," Saidah demanded.

"Why dooz you wat my cell phun fa?" Michelle said, slurring her words even more.

Kirsten just looked at Michelle and shook her head. "I can't believe this," Kirsten said.

"Give me your phone, Michelle," Saidah insisted. "I'm going to call Matt and ask him if he's cheating on you."

"WHAT?" Kirsten asked.

"Noooooo! Matt wift bez mad."

"This girl is so drunk!" Saidah said,

grabbing Michelle's phone out of her jacket pocket, and calling her husband, Matt.

"Matt, are you cheating on Michelle?" was all that Saidah said when he answered the phone."

"WHAT? Is this Saidah?" he asked.

Kirsten grabbed the phone from Saidah, giving her a dirty look.

"Hey, Matt! This is Kirsten."

"What's going on over there, Kirsten?"

"Well, Michelle is upset be—"

"Why you dun lof me no mo. I was a guud wift, Matt. I wuz guud, wasn't I?" Michelle cried out to Matt while Kirsten was trying to explain to him what was going on.

"Kirsten, what is wrong with Michelle?" he asked nervously.

"Matt, I'm sorry to bother you with all of

this. I know how much you love Michelle, but she seems to think you're cheating on her."

"WHAT? WHERE WOULD SHE GET A STUPID IDEA LIKE THAT? LET ME SPEAK TO HER."

"I can't bear to speak," Michelle yelled out, sobbing and rolling over in the dirt.

"Is she drunk?" Matt asked.

"Unfortunately, so," Kirsten responded. "Michelle said you get phone calls from some lady and whenever the lady calls, you make up reasons to leave the house."

Matt started laughing so hard that he was crying. "I'm sorry, I'm sorry. Hold on," he said, still laughing uncontrollably.

All the girls sat there staring at the phone, waiting for Matt to gather his composure. After a minute or so of nonstop laughter, he finally calmed down.

"Kirsten," he said, still trying to keep from laughing. "I'm having Michelle's dream house built. I wanted it to be a surprise. The woman that keeps calling me is my realtor giving me updates on the house. I leave the house when she calls because I'm going to the house to meet with the builders or to see if they are doing everything correctly. I had no idea she was even paying that much attention to me," he said, still fighting back tears of laughter. "Awww, my baby is jealous. I knew I still had it. But, no! I'm not cheating on Michelle. I can't even believe she thought that."

Kirsten and Saidah let out a loud laugh, but Michelle was flabbergasted.

"What did he say?" she asked.

"He's building you your dream house, do-

do bird. He was trying to surprise you. You got me all riled up for nothing!" Saidah said, hitting Michelle upside the head and snatching her up off the ground.

"MY DREAM HOUSE?" Michelle yelled, grabbing the phone from Kirsten. "MATT, ARE YOU LYING?" she asked, sounding like she was miraculously sober.

"Of course, I'm not lying. All you ever do is talk about your dream house. I just want to give it to you, that's all. How could you think I would cheat on you? There is nothing that's worth me losing you and my babies over, believe that!"

"Awww, that's so sweet," Saidah said.

"I knew he wouldn't cheat on you," said Kirsten.

"I'll show you the house when you come

home, okay? Now, please stop drinking," Matt

requested.

"Okay, I'm so sorry, honey," she

responded. "I love you."

"I love you too, babe. Enjoy the rest of

your trip, okay?"

"Okay, bye."

"I found us a hotel," Beatriz chimed in,

interrupting their conversation.

"Great! Perfect timing," Michelle said,

running and jumping in her truck to drive to the

hotel.

"Oh, no! You're not driving anywhere.

Give me the keys!" Kirsten demanded.

"Your big belly can't fit behind that

steering wheel, either," Saidah argued. "I'll

drive," she said, snatching the keys from

Michelle and moving Kirsten out of the way of

the door.

Then all of them jumped in and headed to the hotel. They wanted to pretend that they were sad to be leaving the campground, but the truth was, they were all overjoyed to be going to a hotel with warm showers, free Internet, unlimited television, and no more cheating husband sob stories.

Chapter 19

The next morning at the hotel, everyone hustled and bustled to get showered and dressed to go downtown for lunch and then drive up to Manchester, Tennessee, for a music and art festival.

"Do you have my comb?" Beatriz asked Saidah.

"Have I ever used your comb, Beatriz?"

"I don't know. You've done a lot of things that I don't know about."

"Yes, I sure have, but using your comb wasn't one of them."

"Has anyone seen my toothbrush?"
Michelle yelled.

"Has anyone seen my razor?" Saidah
asked.

While everyone looked for their lost things,
Kirsten just flopped down on the bed with a
bizarre look on her face. Beatriz looked over at
her.

"Are you okay?"

"Yeah, I'm fine," Kirsten responded, but it
was apparent that she wasn't.

"What's wrong?" Michelle asked.

"Nothing! I'm fine," Kirsten snapped.

"No, you're not!" Michelle snapped back,
walking into the bathroom to continue looking
for her toothbrush. Eventually she gave up and
started brushing her teeth with her fingers.

"Are you really brushing your teeth with

your fingers?" Saidah asked her.

"Oh, don't act like you've never used your fingers to brush your teeth when you didn't have a toothbrush. Gosh, I hate uppity people!" Michelle said.

"I'm not uppity and no, I've never used my fingers to brush my teeth, because I've always had a toothbrush," Saidah answered sarcastically.

"WHAT-EVVVVV," Michelle replied, vigorously rubbing her fingers across her teeth like they were just as efficient as a toothbrush.

"Lacey is so unhealthy for Jason. I don't understand why he would want to take her back after all she's done to him," Kirsten said offhandedly.

The entire room became totally quiet as all the ladies stood there in a frozen position staring at her. That was until Michelle yelled, "I KNOW

YOU'RE NOT TALKING ABOUT THAT LYING,

CHEATING, EMOTIONALLY ABUSIVE, NO

GOOD, LOW DOWN, DIRTY SCOUNDREL OF AN

EX-BOYFRIEND, JASON!"

"Don't start, Michelle!" Kirsten huffed. "I

just don't understand why he's remarrying her,

when he obviously doesn't want to."

"How do you know he doesn't want to?"

asked Beatriz.

"Because he told me?"

"Are you still communicating with him?"

asked Saidah.

"No, no! He stopped by my job the other

day and asked me to tell him not to marry

Lacey. He wanted to know if we still had a

chance."

"Is he stupid or what? Didn't Everett put

him in the hospital not too long ago because he wouldn't leave you alone?" Michelle mentioned.

"Wait! What? When did Everett put Jason in the hospital?" asked Beatriz.

"Nothing, nothing! It was a long time ago and it was a nightmare! Please don't talk about that, Michelle," Kirsten pleaded.

"IT WAS JUST LAST YEAR!" Michelle snitched. "That numb nut kissed Kirsten and put his hand up her skirt. Then this crazy fool went home and told her husband as if he wasn't going to retaliate. Everett popped up at Jason's restaurant and started beating him in front of all his employees. Everett went to jail and crazy Jason ended up bailing him out because he felt bad. Girl, the whole situation is nothing but drama! It's ridiculous!"

"MICHELLE! STOP! I'm trying to forget

any of that happened," Kirsten said angrily.

"O.M. Freak'in G! This is a real life soap opera!" Saidah said. "I knew Everett had some bad guy in him, though!"

"STOP IT!" yelled Kirsten. "Everett is wonderful!"

"Yeah, wonderfully gangsta," Saidah joked.

"Kirsten, how could you keep all of this from us? And why would Jason come back to your job after Everett already tried to kill him?" asked Beatriz.

"No, the real question is, why is she crying over Jason marrying another woman? That's the question I need answered," Michelle said in an aggravated tone. "That is not Jason's baby, is it, Kirsten?"

"NO! I can't believe you asked me that!"

"Well, we can't believe you're ruining our

trip by talking about that bird brain. However, since the damage is done, please tell us everything that happened when he came to your office," said Saidah, jumping on the bed beside Kirsten.

"And, don't leave out one detail," Michelle added, as they all gathered on the bed with their legs folded like they were about to listen to a good bedtime story.

"Okay," Kirsten said, agreeing to tell them the full story. "It was a typical day at work. I was sitting at my desk talking to Everett on the phone," she said, as she allowed her mind to drift back to the scandalous scene that took place in her office that rainy afternoon...

"What do you think about leaving work a little early today and we'll go catch a movie or something?" Everett suggested to Kirsten.

"Everett, you've never asked me to skip out on work before. So, you wait until you're almost forty to start living on the edge?"

"I'm almost thirty-nine, thank you very much and yeah, I just feel like seeing my beautiful wife."

"Awww, well okay. But it's raining outside."

"Even better. Maybe we'll go kiss in the rain like they do in the movies or something."

Kirsten laughed and said, "Okay. Let me finish up here and I'll—"

"Kirsten, I need you to tell me that I shouldn't marry Lacey," Jason said, bursting into her office.

"Ms. Larson, I tried to stop him, but he walked right past my desk," Mandy, the receptionist said in a fearful and aggravated tone.

"Ummm, honey. I have to go. I'll call you when I'm on my way," Kirsten said, trying to rush off the phone with Everett.

"What's going on, Kirsten? Who are all those people in your office?"

"Uhhhh, I'll try to explain later. Okay?"

"Ooookkkkaaaay."

"I love you," Kirsten said, slamming the phone down.

"Jason, what is wrong with you? You can't just barge into my office whenever you want, ya know? Just because you're Jason Glaznyte, doesn't mean rules do not apply to you."

"You're THE Mr. Jason B. Glaznyte? Oh! My! Gosh! I've heard so much about you," Mandy said, vigorously shaking his hand.

Jason looked over at Kirsten as if she had been talking about him to Mandy.

Kirsten rolled her eyes.

"It wasn't through me, silly. I don't mention your name AT ALL."

"Kirsten, I'm about to make a huge decision and I need to know how you feel about it," Jason said, trying to redirect their attention. Then he looked back at Mandy, who was standing there, still giving him goo-goo eyes.

"Can I have a minute with Kirsten, please?" he asked nicely.

"NO!" Kirsten blurted out.

"Sure," Mandy said, "But may I have your autograph before you leave?"

"No problem," he said.

Kirsten gave Mandy one of the dirtiest looks known to man.

"What?" Mandy said, frowning at Kirsten. "Just because you don't appreciate having a superstar in your office, doesn't mean that I'm supposed to feel the same."

"Bye, Mandy," Kirsten said sneeringly.

"Bah-Bye," Mandy responded, closing the door behind her.

Kirsten looked at Jason, who was staring at her like she was syrup and he was a biscuit.

"Kirsten, I don't want to make another mistake. If you tell me that there is still a chance for us to be together, I will call off this wedding with Lacey, today."

"JASON, STOP IT! I'm happily married to Everett," she said, standing up and showing Jason her five-months pregnant belly. "And we are expecting our first child," she added.

Jason's eyes widened.

"There is no more US, Jason. It's over. I thought you had come to grips with that. I thought you—"

"I will raise this baby like it's mine. I will be a father to your child, just like you were a mother to mine."

Kirsten looked at Jason like that was the last thing she expected to hear. Her eyes filled with water. She was speechless, immediately reminiscing about how good she was to Jason's son, Ryan. She thought about how much Ryan loved her and how she loved him like she'd given birth to him herself.

"Please, Kirsten! The only thing that matters to me is us being a family."

"Jason, I am already a part of another family with—"

"Just say yes and I'll pay for your divorce.

He can have everything. You don't even have to work anymore if you don't want to. You can stay home and raise our children and I'll give you anything your heart could ever ask for. Just tell me yes, Kirsten, and I will call off this wedding with Lacey."

"Jason, do you remember when we were dating and I told you that I can't save you from Lacey? Well, I still can't save you from her. You chose her over me, so—"

"NO! I never chose her over you. That was a very complicated situation. She was my ex-wife and the mother of my child. I just wanted my family back."

"Well, now, you are getting your family back, so why are you here in my office? See, people always want what they can't have. It's the thrill of conquering and once you've conquered it, you no longer want it."

"That is not true, Kirsten, and you know it. I have always loved you."

"That wasn't love, Jason. You cheated on me with Lacey the entire time we were together. You were about to sleep with her on my birthday, and you would have turned right around and slept with me too, had I not come home and caught y'all in the —NO, NO!" Kirsten said, stopping herself in the middle of her sentence. "I'm not rehashing this with you. Yes, you should marry Lacey! Y'all deserve each other, now please get out of my office."

"Kirsten, please don't kick me out. I was very confused back then."

"No, Jason! You're just confused, period! I do not want the life of drama and insecurity that you keep offering me. My faithful, loyal, drama-free husband wants to take me out for a movie, so if you'll excuse me, I'm going to go and spend time with him. Please do not show up at my office again. If I told Everett that you came here, you know he would kill you!"

"You're not going to tell him, because you still love me," Jason said, giving Kirsten a seductive grin. His light brown eyes seemed to pierce through her soul, immediately giving her flashbacks of the first time they made love. As she thought of Jason, chills shot through her body, then suddenly, her baby kicked, forcing her out of her lustful contemplations.

Kirsten paused and looked at Jason.

"Congratulations on your marriage! I wish you and Lacey the best," she said opening the door for Jason to leave.

"Can I at least have a hug before I go?"

"No, No!" she said, abruptly shaking her head as fast as she could. "Please leave, Jason," she said, refusing to make eye contact with him.

As he walked towards the door, he stopped in front of her and said, "There's nothing you can ever say or do that will make me stop loving and wanting you, Kirsten. I don't care how many kids you have or how long you stay married or how many times you get married, I will always be ready for you to come back to me," he said, then walked off without giving Kirsten a chance to respond or Mandy the autograph he promised.

When Kirsten got ready to leave to go meet Everett, Mandy twisted her lips to one side.

"Hmmm, I didn't get my autograph from Mr. Wonderful. Maybe you can get it for me the next time you two lovebirds meet, and in return

I'll just keep my mouth shut when your husband comes to see you," Mandy said, laughing.

Kirsten stopped and turned around.

"I'm just kidding, Mrs. Larson, geez! I'm just kidding," Mandy expressed.

There were no words to describe the look Kirsten gave Mandy, but Mandy knew if she mentioned anything to Everett about Jason Glaznyte, not only would she not have a job anymore, she would probably come up missing.

"Snitches end up in ditches, Mandy," assured Kirsten.

Mandy let out a huge gasp and her eyes bugged out. "UUUUUHHHHHH! Did you just threaten me?" she asked.

Kirsten gave her a slightly evil grin, then walked away to spend the rest of her day with her wonderful husband, Everett...

Chapter 20

"And that's exactly what happened, every detail," Kirsten said, as she told her friends the entire story of what happened in her office that day.

Beatriz just looked at Kirsten and shook her head.

"Don't judge me, Beatriz!" Kirsten snarled.

Saidah looked over at Beatriz as if they could read each other's mind. There was no need for Saidah to actually say what she was thinking, because Beatriz gave her a nod as if she was agreeing with whatever thought Saidah had in her head.

The room was dead silent until Kirsten blurted out, "NO! NOOO! You guys, stop reading into this! I don't want to be with him. I am happily married to the most wonderful man in the universe. I was just saying that —"

"You can fool Everett, but you can't fool us, Kirsten," Saidah said with her hands on her hips.

"You guys just don't understand the point I'm trying to make! I'm not jealous and I don't want him back. I just don't understand why he's doing something so stupid! Lacey gave up custody of her own son. She dropped her son off at Jason's house with all his clothes and toys packed up in black trash bags. Then she had the audacity to dump all of those black trash bags on Jason's lawn. I moved in with him and took care of Ryan like he was my own son. I became a mother to him because he had no mother. Now, after all of that, Jason is going to marry her again? I just don't understand why he would take her back, that's all."

Beatriz looked at Kirsten and said, "Honey, it is honestly none of your business. He can marry whomever he wants to marry. You are pregnant with your first child. Please focus on that. Please focus on the blessing God has given you and release the past that He's delivered you from. It doesn't matter why Jason is remarrying Lacey. Just be thankful that he didn't marry you."

"What is that supposed to mean?" Kirsten asked, like she was offended.

"Ugggghhhhh!!!!" Michelle moaned! "Duh! Just be happy that you're not the one stuck with him and all of his drama. That's what she means!"

"Yes," agreed Saidah. "He is someone else's problem, not yours, and you should be thankful for that. All he did was cause you pain. I really hope you're not one of those people who are attracted to drama, Kirsten, because God doesn't send us unhealthy people or unhealthy relationships."

"Says who?" Kirsten refuted.

"Kirsten is right, Saidah," Beatriz agreed. "God can send you any kind of person He chooses!"

"Just forget this whole conversation!" said Kirsten, obviously agitated. "No one knows what I'm trying to say!"

"What we know is," Michelle said, chiming in. "You're married to a good looking, hardworking, faithful man who loves God and loves you more than anything and you're over here depressed because your ex doggie, ruff, ruff, Rufus is about to remarry his crazy ex-wife. We should be out having fun right now instead of dealing with this nonsense."

Saidah laughed out loud. "EX DOGGIE RUFF, RUFF RUFUS," she screamed, still laughing.

"Look, I didn't mean it the way it came out. I'm happily married and I would never give Everett up for anyone. Jason can marry whomever he wants, okay? Can we get dressed and leave now?" Kirsten asked.

"YES!!!" all three ladies screamed as each went back to doing whatever they were doing before Kirsten started whining about Jason and Lacey.

"Nothing looks good on me anymore. I hate pregnant clothes," Kirsten complained as she took one last look at herself in the mirror. "And, look at how big my butt has gotten! I can't believe—"

"I will leave you standing right here in that mirror if all you're going to do is complain," Saidah threatened.

Just then there was a knock at the hotel door. "Oh, that must be Melah," Kirsten said, running and opening the door.

"Hey, girl! I didn't think you were going to make it," Kirsten said, giving Melah a hug.

"Hmmmm," Michelle grumbled.

"Well, I wasn't sure if I was going to be too tired to drive up here after we got back in town, but Daniel drove the whole time, so I was well rested. Thank you for inviting me."

"Hmmm Mmmm," Michelle grumbled again.

Kirsten and Melah both looked over at Michelle.

"This is Melah, everybody."

"Hi Melah. It's nice to meet you," Beatriz and Saidah said, while Michelle acted like she was still busy dancing in the bathroom mirror.

"THIS IS MELAH, MICHELLE!" Kirsten said, leaning over and looking directly at Michelle.

"Oh, hi, Melah. I didn't know you were here; I was listening to music on my headphones."

All the girls just shook their heads at Michelle, but Melah didn't seem to think anything of it.

"So what did I miss?" Melah asked

excitedly.

"Nothing at all," Kirsten said. "We were just getting ready to head out to dinner, then up to Manchester for a musical and art festival."

"That is great! I am starving!" Melah replied, "But I thought we were going to a campground."

No one said a word.

"Tell Melah about the campground, guys," Beatriz blurted out.

"It was horrible and we hated it," Michelle responded.

Melah laughed. "Awww, I love going camping. I hate I missed that."

Beatriz ran and gave Melah a hug. "I'm so glad you're here. Maybe you and I can go to the campground tonight or tomorrow. Whadda ya say?"

"I'd love to. Let's do it," Melah responded enthusiastically.

Michelle and Saidah both gave Kirsten a dirty look because Melah was all the encouragement Beatriz needed to try and make them go camping again. Kirsten shrugged her shoulders and mouthed an "I'm sorry" to both of them.

"Are you guys ready?" Beatriz asked, still showing how excited she was to have Melah around.

"Yes, let's go," Melah said, as she and Beatriz walked out of the hotel room laughing and giggling like they had a kindred connection.

Kirsten happily joined their bond, while Saidah and Michelle begrudgingly walked behind them, doing their best to not act like Melah had just come and taken their best friends away from them.

When they got to the restaurant, Saidah had become as jealous as Michelle over Melah and neither of them were showing any Southern hospitality. At first, Melah tried to blow it off, but then she got fed up with their smart comments and them disagreeing with everything she said.

"What is the problem?" Melah blurted out to Saidah and Michelle. "Did I do something to you?"

"You didn't do anything to them," Beatriz reassured her. "They are not open-minded individuals and they don't like change," she said with an attitude.

"What does that have to do with me? I can tell that they clearly have a problem with me," she said, staring at Saidah and Michelle.

"Yeah, I do have a problem with you coming up here and acting like you and my best friend are best friends. I don't like that. You don't even know her like I know her," Saidah feuded.

"And you?" Melah asked, looking at Michelle.

"Ditto to what she just said," Michelle responded.

Melah looked over at Kirsten and Beatriz who both had their heads down like they were embarrassed.

"Oh, we're going to get along just fine," Melah said to Michelle and Saidah. "Y'all both have Type A personalities, so you know how to speak your mind. I am Type A too, so I can appreciate where you're coming from. I'll forgive y'all for being so rude to me if y'all will forgive me for barging into your already formed bond,

and taking your friends."

"You don't have to apologize for that,

Melah. I invited you to come," said Kirsten.

"Yeah," agreed Beatriz.

"HUSH," Saidah said. "Let the woman

finish apologizing. I think I'm starting to like

her."

Michelle laughed. "I'm sorry too, Melah. I

was just jealous. Can we start over?"

"Absolutely!" Melah said like she wouldn't

have it any other way.

"Good," Saidah said, as the ladies ate their

lunch, then went off to enjoy the rest of their

week together. Beatriz and Melah even talked

them into going back to the campground, but

this time they stayed all night, and Michelle

didn't get drunk and accuse her husband of

cheating.

By the end of the week, this group of four had willingly expounded their boundaries to become a seemingly perfect group of five.

Chapter 21

As the girls ended their trip and all went back to their separate lives, Kirsten could not wait to get back to church on Sunday; she was hoping the homeless guy would return, so she could find out more about him, but he wasn't there. And the next Sunday came and he still wasn't there. As each Sunday, passed, she did not see him. She and Everett said a prayer for him that he would be okay and that no harm would come to him.

In the meanwhile, Kirsten saw in the local newspaper that her ex-boyfriend, Jason had gotten remarried. She tried to be happy for them, but she couldn't. She knew Jason was making a terrible mistake. There was no way he was going to be happy with Lacey, and unfortunately for Kirsten, her intuition was correct. What she didn't know, though, was how Jason's terrible mistake was about to change her life forever...

One day, Jason was busy at work. It was 3:00 p.m. and he had been in meetings since the moment he walked through the door that morning.

"I've had enough. I'm going home," he said to his receptionist. Just as he was about to head home for the evening, he received a strange phone call from his wife, Lacey.

"Jason, do you love me more than you love Kirsten?" Lacey asked abruptly, as soon as

Jason said hello.

"Don't do this Lacey. We have a son to raise and we got remarried so we could raise him together. This is what we both wanted and agreed to, remember?"

"I remember when you loved me more than anything or anyone. Do you remember that?" she asked somberly. "Let's go for a walk before we go home this evening," she suggested.

"Lacey, why do we need to walk before we go home? Why can't we go home, get Ryan and we all go for a walk together?"

"No!" she snapped. I just want to walk and talk with my husband. Is that okay? Just the two of us; you know how much I love being in your big, strong arms," she said, changing her tone from psycho to flirtatious.

He could tell that Lacey was smiling.

"Okay," he said hesitantly.

"Meet me by the nature trail down by Swan Lane," she said excitedly.

"Swan Lane? Lacey, that's way out in the boon docks. Why do we have to go so far out into the country when there's a really nice nature trail right up the street from us?"

"Jason, please!" Lacey huffed. "It would really mean a lot to me, okay?"

"Okay! Alright! Fine! I'll meet you there in 15 minutes."

"Thank you, sweetheart. I'm going to give you something you will never forget," she said, with a frisky grin.

Jason pretended to giggle. "I can't wait," he responded as he hung up the phone.

Although I really wish I could wait, he thought to himself as he got into his top of the line Mercedes and drove off to meet Lacey, complaining to himself all the way there.

Why do we need to go for a walk? All she wants to do is complain about how I don't love her, how I never wanted to marry her, and how I still love Kirsten. I don't wanna hear that! I remarried her, didn't I? Why does any of that other stuff matter? I'm tired! I've worked all day and I just want to go home, eat, shower and go to bed for goodness sake, but NOOOOOOO, she has me driving to the country to go for a stupid walk that's not going to change one thing in our screwed up marriage! he thought.

Jason went on and on and on until he reached the trail where Lacey was patiently waiting on him.

"Hey, baby! I'm so glad you came," she said, giving him a kiss.

She noticed that he didn't really kiss her back.

"What's wrong?" she asked.

"Nothing. I just don't know why we have to go for a walk before we go home. Good thing I had a change of clothes in the car," he grumbled.

"Stop complaining! Come on. It'll be fun," she said, standing there dressed in some tiny mint green shorts that were struggling to cover her butt.

"Why are you dressed like that? I thought you went to work today?"

"Oh, I did. I had a change of clothes in the car too," she said, grabbing his hands and pulling him into the woods.

He looked around, immediately noticing how quiet it was there. It was almost spooky,

264

but he had complained so much that he decided to try and relax and just go with the flow.

"I've always loved you," Lacey said, looking up at Jason, who seemed to be deep in thought.

"Jason, are you listening?"

"Yeah, yeah!"

"Well, what did I say?"

"I'm listening and I know you love me."

"No, I've always loved you."

"Okay, so wh—"

"I know you thought that I didn't, but I did. It's just that I never knew how to love. My childhood was pretty rough, ya know?"

"Yeah, I know, baby, but—"

"And unfortunately people who are hurt, hurt others. That's what I did to you. I hurt you Jason and I'm sorry."

"It's fine, Lacey. It's in the past and—"

"I'm also sorry for any hurt I may cause you in the future," she said, as they walked deeper into the woods.

"Lacey, you don't have to apologize. We will be fine. Let's go home and I'll take you out to dinner, alright?" Jason said, trying to persuade Lacey to end their weird nature walk.

"Don't try to pretend, Jason! I know our marriage is not going to last," she said coldly.

Jason stopped dead in his tracks and looked in Lacey's eyes. He knew something had changed. It seemed like something had suddenly taken control of Lacey.

"Are you okay?" he asked hesitantly. "I think we should go home now."

"FOR WHAT?" she yelled, piercingly.

As big and as strong as Jason was over Lacey, fear rippled through his body. He stood there speechless as flames of fire seemed to overtake Lacey's eyes. She composed herself and calmly asked, "Why can't you get over Kirsten? What does she do for you that I don't do?"

"Lacey, Kirsten and I have been over for a very long time, why do you keep bringing her up?" he asked calmly, walking backwards out of the woods.

"WELL, WHY DID YOU GO TO HER OFFICE THE DAY BEFORE WE GOT MARRIED?"

"Whoa, Lacey. Calm down, now. Don't go assuming anything."

"I saw you, Jason. Each day, for a whole week, you circled the parking lot of her office building, trying to build up the nerve to go in and talk to her. Then one day, you stop circling and went in. I watched the whole thing unfold."

"You were following me?"

Lacey laughed. "Of course I followed you. I knew you would eventually go see her. You asked her to marry you and she said no, didn't she? Is that why you married me?"

"Come on, Lacey. Don't do this out here. Let's just—"

"ANSWER THE QUESTIION, JASON!"

"NOOOOO! I did not ask her to marry me!"

"I know you don't love me. You only married me for Ryan. Ever since Kirsten came into the picture, your love for me vanished," Lacey said, staring out into the woods.

"That's not true! Don't jump to conclusions, Lacey, and don't do anything stupid, alright?" he said holding both of his hands in front of Lacey to keep a distance between them.

"Well, tell me you love me more than her. TELL ME!" she screamed as loud as she could. Her voice echoed through the woods. "Tell me you want me, Jason. Tell me I'm the only woman for you. WHY AREN'T YOU TELLING ME, JASON?" she screamed again. "You can't tell me can you?" she asked, going from violent to calm all in one breath.

"Lacey, you know I love you. You know I want you, but I'm not going to do this with you out here."

"So, you love me?"

"Yes, I love—"

"LIAR! I know you don't love me," she said, as she pulled a gun out of her pocket and pointed it at him.

"Oh God! Lacey don't do this. We have a son who loves us dearly. If you kill me, you're going to go to jail and he won't have anyone."

"Oh, don't worry, he'll be alright! You and little Ms. Kirsten did a fine job raising him. I'm sure she will happily petition the courts to gain custody of him. Besides, he loves her more than he loves me anyway. Like father, like son!" Lacey said. "And how's your new addition?" she inquired.

"WHAT? What are you talking about?"

"The baby she's carrying, dummy! Oh, you thought I didn't know that she was pregnant, didn't you?"

"That is not my child, Lacey. Kirsten is happily married!"

"Such a liar! You and I both know that Kirsten is not happily married, Jason! So, are y'all hoping for a little girl this time or will she have a boy and name him after you?   I know you've always wanted a junior, haven't you?" Then she looked Jason directly into his eyes.

"She can have Ryan, she can even have this baby, but I will never let her have you!" she said, pulling the trigger, barely missing his heart.

"Uuuuuuuhhhhhhhhhhhh!" Jason gasped for air as he fell to the ground.

"All I wanted was for you to love me," she whispered. You knew I needed love. You knew I never had anyone! YOU WERE SUPPOSED TO LOVE ME!" she screamed, breaking down into tears.

She hovered over Jason's beautiful, dark chocolate body as he lay there in his blood.

"Dang, you're fine! It's too bad you had to

die," she said, placing the gun back in her pocket, so she could leave him there to die.

Her get-away plan was perfectly orchestrated. First, she will go back to Jason's car and make it look like a carjacking. Then she will drive to Miami to meet her lover of fifteen years. When she reaches Miami, she will call the babysitter and ask to speak to Jason. When the babysitter tells her that Jason never came home that night, she will act belligerent, accuse him of cheating, and beg the babysitter to stay with Ryan until she returns from her "business" trip, which will give her a perfect alibi. Once authorities notify her of Jason's death, she will sob uncontrollably, cash in on his insurance policy, collect all of her inheritance, then pretend to have a nervous breakdown while attending the funeral. Afterwards, she will claim that she needs to get away for a few days to clear

her head. She'll fly to another country, leaving

Ryan in the loving and capable hands of his

babysitter, never to return again. Her plan was

foolproof, or so she thought.

As she lifted her foot to step over Jason's

dying body, he grabbed her leg, causing her to

trip and fall. She pulled the gun back out of her

pocket, but he knocked it out of her hand. She

kicked him in his groin area and he balled up in

a fetal position. She started crawling towards

the gun, but he grabbed her leg again. She

kicked him in the face, but somehow he

managed to crawl on top of her and pin her

down. She could smell his seductive cologne,

even in the midst of the blood continuing to spill

from his body.

"Why are you trying to kill me?" he

muttered, still pinning her to the ground in hopes of blocking the open wound in his chest.

"I refuse to live with you knowing your heart is with another woman. Next time, I'll make sure I kill you," she proclaimed, hitting him in the head with a rock.

Jason had never hit a woman before, but this time he'd have to make an exception. He had lost a lot of blood, and was very weak, but there was no way he was going to let Lacey leave him there to die.

He jumped up, still bleeding. He ran towards the gun and she ran behind him, jumping on his back and putting him in a choke hold. He slammed her up against a tree and body slammed her onto the ground, but when he did, blood splattered everywhere. Unbeknownst to him, her head hit a sharp object and it cracked her skull open. Lacey immediately

became limp. Jason looked over at her; he knew

that she was dead. He wanted to cry, but he

knew his life would also be in danger if he didn't

get to a hospital. He was growing somewhat

disoriented, but did his best to find his way out

of the woods. He made it back to his car, which

was parked near the highway. As he opened the

door to get in, he passed out from all the blood

loss.

About 20 minutes later a man drove by

and saw Jason lying on the ground and his car

door opened. He immediately called the

ambulance and stayed there with Jason until

they arrived, but it was too late. Jason was

pronounced dead at the scene.

When Jason nor Lacey showed up at the

house that evening, their babysitter called the

cops. They told her that they fit the names and description of a couple that had been found dead that day, but they were still investigating the scene. The investigator asked if she could provide him with numbers to their next of kin.

"I don't have their next of kin information, but there is a filing cabinet in Mr. Glaznyte's office. One day, I saw him reviewing his will and he placed it in there. Would you like me to get it for you?" she asked.

"That would be very helpful ma'am. We will be sending someone out to the home to confiscate that if you don't mind."

"No, not at all. I have his son here with me. Should I take him to my house for the night?"

"Given the severity of this case, that might be a good idea."

"Ummm, ok," she said and went to pack up Ryan's things.

It wasn't long before several cop cars showed up with a warrant to search the Glaznyte property.

"What's going on?" Ryan asked. "Why are so many cops here?"

"Oh, I think there's about to be a parade in the neighborhood, sweetie and they're here to escort everyone."

"No there isn't," Ryan said as if he didn't believe one word she was saying.

"You're gonna spend the night with me, okay?" she said to Ryan.

"Why? Where are my parents?"

"They had to go somewhere, and they need you to stay with me, okay honey?"

Ryan got in the car and sat there staring

out of the window at all the cops taking things out of his parents' house. The babysitter went to talk to one of the cops.

"Here's a copy of the will y'all asked me to give you," she said to the cop.

"Thank you. Where is the little boy?"

"He's in my car."

"Go ahead and get him outta here, but leave me your number; we may have more questions," the cop said.

"Okay," she said hesitantly like she didn't want anything to do with what was taking place, but she gave them her number and she and Ryan headed to her house.

Chapter 22

♫ ♪ ♫ *Ding dong, ding dong, ding dong,* ♫ ♪ ♫ the babysitter heard early the next morning.

"Someone is at your door," Ryan said.

The babysitter slowly opened the door.

"Hi, can I help you?" she asked the lady standing on her porch.

"Yes, I'm Ms. Joan Holiday. I work for the Child Protective Services for this region. I was told that you have the son of Jason and Lacey Glaznyte in your custody. Is that correct?"

"Do you know my parents?" Ryan asked.

Ms. Holiday smiled. "No, sweetheart, I don't, but I'm here to take you to a new home, okay?"

"Why do I need to go to a new home?" Ryan asked.

"Well, baby. There was an incident with your parents and they both passed away, so you have to go live in a new home, but I think you will really like it."

"So when are my parents coming to pick me up?" he asked.

Ms. Holiday looked over at the babysitter.

"Well, sweetie, they have passed. Do you know what that means?"

"No."

"Well, it means they both died, honey. Do you know what that means?'

"Oh! Yeah, I know what that means,"

Ryan said, acting like he was still confused.

"I'm going to take you to a new home, okay?"

"Okay," he said grabbing his bag of toys, hugging his babysitter goodbye, and heading out of the door with Ms. Holiday.

They drove up to this beautiful brick home and Ms. Holiday parked her car. "Stay here with this nice police officer while I make a quick stop," she told Ryan, as a cop walked over to the car to sit with him until she returned.

"BAM, BAM, BAM, BAM," Everett heard at his front door while he was trying to take a nap.

"GRRRRRRR!" Everett mumbled at the thought of his sleep being interrupted.

When he looked out of the window, he saw a cop car, then another car with a cop sitting on the passenger side. He opened the door.

"Yes, how can I help you?" Everett asked hesitantly.

"Sorry to beat on your door so hard, but I've been knocking for quite a while and it's very important that I speak with you."

"How long have you been knocking?"

"At least five minutes," Ms. Holiday said.

"Oh, was that you? I thought I was dreaming," Everett responded with a smile.

She laughed, then quickly got to the reason why she was there.

"I'm looking for Kirsten Jabard. Does she live here?" she asked politely.

"Yes, but she is Kirsten Larson now; she's my wife. What is this about?"

The lady gave Everett a weird stare.

"I'm sorry, but I really need to speak with your wife. Can you tell me where I can find her?"

"I don't know," Everett said with an attitude. "What do you need her for?"

Just then Kirsten pulled up into the driveway. She got out of the car and ran towards Everett.

"Is everything okay?" she asked frantically.

"Are you Kirsten Jabard?" the lady asked.

"Well, I'm Kirsten Larson now, but Jabard is my maiden name."

"Great! I'm Ms. Joan Holiday. I'm new to this region; I work with Child Protective Services. Do you mind if I come in and talk to you for a minute?"

"Sure, but what is this about?"

"Do you know someone by the name of Jason Glaznyte?"

"Uhhhmm," Kirsten responded.

Everett interrupted. "Yeah, she knows him. Now what is this about?"

Kirsten eyes got big and Everett sat there with an angry look on his face.

"Well," Ms. Holiday said, letting out a long sigh. "Mr. Glaznyte and his wife have both been killed, and in his will you have been appointed as guardian over his son, Ryan."

"What?" Kirsten asked shockingly.

"You've got to be kidding me," Everett said.

"Wait! Jason and Lacey are both dead?" Kirsten asked, sounding utterly confused.

"And Jason appointed you as guardian over Ryan," Everett added, while shaking his head.

"Well, actually he appointed her as guardian over everything, including his son," Ms. Holiday said, looking at Everett.

Why am I not surprised, Everett thought.

"But, what about Lacey? He was married to her. Surely she wouldn't agree to me having custody of Ryan," inquired Kirsten.

"It appears that the will was notarized before they got remarried. At the time, he had full custody of Ryan, and nothing was changed afterwards. He has left everything to you."

"What do you mean, everything?"

"That is out of my lane, Mrs. Jaba—I mean Mrs. Larson. I'm only here to talk about the well-being of Ryan, but I'm sure you'll be hearing something really soon about the remainder of Mr. Glaznyte's estate."

"I can't believe this," Kirsten said, looking over at Everett, who was giving her a blank stare.

"I love Ryan like he's my own son, but it's

not just me anymore, Ms. Holiday. This is a decision I need to talk with my husband about. Can you give us a few minutes to talk?"

"There's nothing to talk about," Everett said.

Kirsten let out a small gasp.

"Of course we will raise Ryan," Everett added, nodding his head "yes" to Ms. Holiday.

Kirsten gave him a strange look.

"Are you sure you are okay with this, Everett?"

"This little boy has just lost both of his parents and regardless of who his parents are, or how I feel about them, Ryan loves you like a mother and you love him like a son. I can't think of a better place for him live than right here...with us," Everett replied.

"And that's why I love you more than

anything," Kirsten said, giving him a big hug and kiss.

"So is that a yes?" Ms. Holiday asked.

"YES!" Kirsten said. "We'll take him! Where is he?"

"He's in the car. I'll go get him," Ms. Holiday said excitedly.

When she brought Ryan into the house, he ran and gave Kirsten a big hug.

"Hey, Mrs. Kirsten! Where have you been?" Ryan asked.

"Oh, I've been around, here and there, but I'm here to stay now."

"Are you going to come to my new home with me?" Ryan asked, and everyone laughed.

"This is your new home, honey. Here with me and Mr. Everett."

"Yippie," Ryan said. "Do you know my

mommy and daddy died?"

"Yeah, I'm so sorry, sweetie."

"They fussed all the time, Mrs. Kirsten. My dad was so unhappy. My mom hated him. She used to tell me that she wished he was dead. I don't think she liked me either," he said.

"Oh," was all Kirsten could say as she looked up at Ms. Holiday and the cop taking notes. "Well, Mr. Everett and I are very happy that you are coming to live with us," she said.

"I'm happy, too," Ryan said, laying happily in Kirsten's arms like he was finally in a place where he felt loved and protected.

Chapter 23

Having Ryan around was just like old times for Kirsten, except Jason was now replaced with Everett. Although Everett hated Jason, Ryan had seemingly won his heart and he looked forward to each day. He used it as a test case to see if he would make a good father when his and Kirsten's baby arrived. They told Ryan that they were expecting and that he would have a baby sister in a few months. Boy was Ryan excited about that!

When Sunday came, Kirsten, Everett and Ryan all went to church. It had been almost two months since they'd seen the homeless guy, so they had given up on ever seeing him again, but to their surprise, when they arrived at church, there he was, sitting on the bench outside of the church, just like the first day he visited.

"HEY!!!!" Kirsten yelled, running over to him like she wanted to give him a hug. Everett came over too, and vigorously shook his hand.

"It's really good to see you, man. We thought you weren't coming back," said Everett.

"Well, I almost didn't!" he said. "One of my friends graduated from high school, and I really wanted to be there, so I hitchhiked up to where he lives. To get up there from here took me a month," he said.

"High school?" How old are you?" Kirsten asked.

"I'm eighteen."

"Eighteen?" they both said.

"Man, we thought you were older than that," said Everett.

"No, I just turned eighteen last week. I was supposed to be graduating this year too, but life happened and here I am, but I definitely wanted to see him walk across that stage. After the graduation ceremony was over, I walked up to him. Of course he didn't know who I was. I looked at him and said, 'Congratulations, man. You've made it,' reaching my hand out to shake his. He stopped and looked at me. Then he gave me the biggest hug ever. I never knew how much I missed him until he hugged me. It didn't even matter what I looked like. It was just like old times. He invited me to his home to take a shower and put on some clean clothes. He even offered me a razor to shave my beard, but I kinda liked my beard, so I only took him up on the shower and the clothes. His parents threw him a huge party and it felt like home to me. Everyone was so happy to see me; they all thought I was dead, but I said, 'Nope, I've just been living the life of luxury in Georgia.' They all laughed. After the party, he and I went out of town to another party that his friends were putting on. We both had something to drink, but neither of us seemed to be drunk. Right before we left, my friend started acting weird, but I thought he was just celebrating his graduation. We were really tired, though, and against our better judgment, we jumped in the car to drive home," the homeless guy said, as he began to sob. "My friend must have fallen asleep at the wheel because the next thing I knew, we hit a ramp."

Kirsten gasped for air.

"The car went flying over the bridge and I woke up, but my friend looked like he was still asleep, but his eyes were partially opened. I kept yelling his name, but he wouldn't wake up. It was like he wasn't even there. I tried to unbuckle my seatbelt, but it was stuck. I eventually got the seatbelt off and tried to open the door so I could jump out, but it was too late. The car hit the water and we began to sink. My window was rolled down a little and the car quickly filled with water. I looked back over at my friend. He had finally woken up, but for some reason, he wasn't fighting for his life. I don't know if he was just too drunk to understand that we were dying or if he just didn't care. I cannot explain what was going through his head, but he clearly wasn't trying to stay alive. I've had too many encounters with

death where I ended up conquering, and right

then and there, I vowed that this encounter

would be no different. I looked at the small hole

in the window. I knew it wasn't big enough for

me to crawl out. I grabbed a hammer from the

pile of tools in my friend's back seat and I

started hitting the window as hard as I could. I

looked over at him, wondering why he wasn't

fighting. He looked like he had fallen back

asleep, so I hit him as hard as I could, then went

back to chipping away at the window. I don't

know how I was able to hold my breath that

long, but I did. 'YOU WILL NOT TAKE MY LIFE!

GOD, PLEASE SAVE ME!' I kept shouting

repeatedly in my head. I may be crazy but it

was like a big shadow came and stood outside of

my window and held it in place so I couldn't

escape. I felt like I was losing consciousness,

but I refused to die. I started kicking the

window as hard as I could and in my head I kept

screaming, 'MOVE! GET OUT OF MY WAY!

YOU WILL NOT TAKE MY LIFE! GOD, PLEASE

SAVE ME!' This went on for what seemed to be

eternity. Then suddenly, the window broke and

the shadow plunged to the bottom of the lake

like someone had pushed it. The next thing I

knew, I woke up on the ground, coughing up

water. There were all of these people around

me, and I had never seen any of them. 'Where is

my friend?' I asked all the people standing there

me, but they just shook their heads. 'I'm sorry.

He didn't make it,' some man said. 'You almost

didn't make it either,' he added. 'But some

people saw your car go over the bridge and they

all worked together to rescue you. Y'all were

under water for so long, that no one thought you would live. It's only by the sweet grace of God that you're here, son. I'm really sorry about your friend. Really, I am,' the man said."

The homeless guy looked up at Everett and Kirsten still crying like a baby. "I told his mom how sorry I was, but the look on her face made it obvious that she didn't forgive me. I told her how I tried to wake him up; how I tried to get him to fight, but it was like I was talking to a brick wall. I told her how weird he was acting before we left the party and maybe that had something to do with the accident, but one of his family members got mad and said I was just trying to cover up what I did. His dad tried to tell me that it was going to be okay, but his eyes were shouting, 'IF YOU HADN'T COME HERE, OUR SON WOULD STILL BE ALIVE.' I didn't even stay for the funeral. I knew I was no longer welcomed there. I loved him like he was my brother. This is the one time I wish God would have taken my life and let my friend live. I just wished my friend would have fought for his life that night. I don't understand why he didn't even try to fight. Why didn't he fight?" he asked, sobbing uncontrollably and placing his head in his lap.

"I wished my dad would have fought for his life too," Ryan said, handing the guy a half used Kleenex that he pulled out of his pocket.

The guy lifted his head and gently grabbed the Kleenex out of Ryan's hands. "Thank you, lil man," he said, wiping his face. He didn't seem to mind that it was already wet. He was used to other people's hand-me-downs. "Is this your aunt and uncle?" he asked Ryan.

"No, they're my new parents," Ryan said. "My real mom and dad died on the same day."

The guy's eyes watered, and once again, he began to sob. He took a deep breath, trying to fight back the tears.

"Both of my parents died on the same day too," he said, wiping his face some more. "I'm so glad God has given you two more wonderful parents, so you don't have to end up like me."

"How did you end up?" asked Ryan.

"Homeless," the man said, crying uncontrollably again. Then he got up off of the bench.

"I just came to tell y'all bye," he said, looking at Everett and Kirsten.

"Where are you going?" Kirsten asked.

"Back to my home town. I never got a chance to say goodbye to my parents, so I'm going to do that and now that I'm eighteen, I can get a job, without Ms. Holiday from Child Protective Services hunting me down."

Everett and Kirsten gave each other a blank stare. They were very thankful that Ryan didn't remember that it was Ms. Holiday who brought him to their house. The looked back at the guy.

"Here's some money," Everett said, reaching into his pocket and pulling out several twenty dollar bills. "This should help you get to wherever you're trying to go."

"Thank you so much. The love you have shown me is the true meaning of what Christianity is all about. I will never forget your generosity," he said, then he looked down at Ryan.

"Take care of yourself, lil man," he said as

he walked away.

They all waved goodbye and Kirsten, Everett and Ryan headed up the steps to go into the church.

"SIR! SIR!" Ryan yelled to the man as he walked down the street.

He stopped, then turned around. "Yes," he said, like he wasn't sure if Ryan was talking to him.

"What is your name? I want to pray and ask God to help you find a new family like he did for me."

The man smiled, as more tears ran down his face.

"Casper! My name is Casper Raine," he said, as he turned back around and walked into the distance until he disappeared.

Chapter 24

Casper took the money and caught a bus as close to his hometown as he could get. Then he caught a ride the rest of the way.

When he finally got there, he smiled. For the first time since his parents had died, he felt like he was safe again. He began thinking about all the things that had happened to him. He thought about the shadow standing by the window underwater. He thought about how he was in a face-to-face stand-off with Death, and once again, Death was defeated!

"God, thank you!" Casper said, knowing

that God had intervened during that encounter, and every other encounter where Death tried to take his life.

"Thank you! Thank you!" Casper began saying, jumping up and down celebrating the life God had given him. "It's been a long road, but I've made it. Sometimes I didn't know what was going to happen to me, but you helped me. Thank you, God. THANK YOU!" he screamed, still jumping up and down. Several cars passed by and stared at him, but he didn't care. He understood that he should have been dead so many times, but it was God and God alone, who was there to help him. At that moment, nothing else mattered. He was back at home and he knew everything was going to be okay. He couldn't wait to go see his parents, even if they were buried in a grave. He was going to tell them how much he missed them and how he

hated that he wasn't able to go to their funeral.

He was going to tell them everything as if they

could hear him. He couldn't wait, but first, he

went to the local funeral home to find out where

they were buried.

"Ummm, hhhhhii," he stuttered, walking

slowly through the front door of the funeral

home, still sweating from all the jumping around

he had done.

"Hi, can we help you?" a lady asked.

"Uh, yeaaahhh," he stuttered some more.

"I'm Casper Raine, I'm trying to find out—"

"Oh my heavens!" the lady said, dropping

the pen she was holding in her hand. She ran

and gave Casper a big hug. I tried to find you,

but no one knew where you went. How are

you?" the lady asked, rubbing Casper's head like

he was a little kid, seemingly not noticing the

sweat pouring off of him, and his dirty and torn

clothes.

"Uhhh, do I know you from somewhere?"

he asked suspiciously, looking at her very

closely. She had dark skin, and her hair was jet

black with a long grey streak in the front.

She laughed, seemingly releasing the sun

from its clouds, with her big bright smile.

"No, I guess you don't," she said, inviting

him to have as seat. "When you were little, your

mom and I used to be very good friends."

Those words caused Casper to let out a

small pant. He felt like he had somehow struck

gold.

"I worked for the bank downtown and I

talked your parents into opening up a college

fund for you. About twelve years ago I retired

from the bank and moved to Pennsylvania to live with my daughter. At first, your mom and I kept in touch, but I moved a few times and we eventually lost contact with each other. One day, out of the blue, I got a call from a mutual friend of mine and your mom. They told me that your parents had died in car accidents and your uncle would not pay to have them buried. Casper, I was furious," the lady said. And although her skin was dark, Casper swore she turned red all over. "I immediately got on a plane and flew down to this funeral home and paid for them to be buried side-by-side. When I—"

"Wait! That's why I came here; I want to know where my parents are buried. Can you take me to see them?"

"Of course I can, but first we need to get

you a bath and some clean clothes on. You don't want your parents to see you looking like that, do you? They would turn over in their grave, child," she said, with a huge grin on her face.

Casper looked down at himself. *I must look horrible,* he thought. *The last time I took a bath was at Kris' house and that was over a month ago.*

Dirty clothes and a smelly body had become the norm for Casper. He looked up at the lady, who was letting him enjoy his inward thoughts. She gave him a slight grin.

"We have a shower in the back. You're welcome to use it," she said. "I'll go look in our pile of clothes to see if we have something that will fit you, okay?"

"Oh, okay! That'll be great. Thank you,"

Casper responded appreciatively, then abruptly said, "Can I ask you something personal about my parents?"

"Yeah, sure you can."

"Do you know what happened between my dad, my grandma and my uncle? Do you know why my dad stopped talking to my grandma?"

The lady looked away, then down at the floor like that was the last thing she expected Casper to ask.

"I know something bad happened; please tell me what it was," Casper asked like he desperately needed some sort of closure to that situation.

She took a few deep breaths as if she was trying to gather her thoughts. Casper sat there patiently waiting for her to give him the pieces to a puzzle that he longed to put together.

"Well," she said, letting out a long sigh. "One day, your parents were having a dinner party. There were people everywhere. Your grandma was supposed to be watching you upstairs, but she fell asleep. While all of the adults were downstairs having fun, your uncle somehow snuck upstairs where you were. He had you in the bathroom and he was trying to make you do something, but you started crying, and he slapped you. When he slapped you, someone was passing by the stairs and heard it. You started screaming your head off. Your uncle was threatening you, saying, 'You better be quiet or else.'

At that time your grandma woke up and everyone downstairs had ran upstairs to see what was going on. Your dad broke the door down and you were standing there naked and so was your uncle. Your grandma hit your uncle with everything she could get her hands on and your dad almost killed him. It was a bloody mess. We ended up calling the cops and your dad pressed charges. You were so little that you couldn't really explain what he had done and there was no physical evidence that he had hurt you. He claimed that he was using the bathroom, then you came in so he was trying to help you sit on the toilet and just became frustrated that you kept whining. He claimed he never slapped you, he just hit his hand on the sink, although the side of your face was red. The cops never arrested your uncle, but it was said that when your grandma questioned him, he started crying and admitted that he had a problem and he had molested you several times before. She confessed this to your dad and he went back to the police station to reopen the case and have your uncle arrested, but your grandma would not testify against him, and with her being the only witness, there was nothing the cops could do."

"Why wouldn't she testify? She just doesn't seem like she would let my uncle get away with something like that."

"Well, rumor has it that her brother used to molest your uncle when he was small. Some people even said he raped him."

"What?"

"Shortly after your grandma and grandpa found out, her brother mysteriously came up missing. To this day, his body has never been found. Folks said your grandparents hired someone to kill him, but no one could ever prove it, and of course, your grandma didn't have a

thing to say about it. That's why folks thought
she was in on it."

"You've got to be kidding me!"

"I wish I was, Casper. Everyone knew that
your grandma felt like it was her fault for not
protecting your uncle from her brother and she
couldn't bring herself to testify against him, even
though she knew he was guilty of molesting you.
She said to your dad, 'If we send him to jail, he's
going to be raped by those men and I can't let
that happen to him,' but your dad didn't care.
All that mattered to him was protecting you, and
since your grandma wasn't willing to do that, he
banned her from ever being around you again.
She tried to assure him that she would never let
your uncle come near you, but that was not
good enough. Your dad changed his phone
number and they moved into another house,

and that was the last time he ever talked to your grandma."

"So, how was she able to get custody of me when my parents passed?"

"Well, your dad didn't have a will appointing anyone as a guardian over you, and your grandma was the next of kin. No one really knew what happened to you. There were so many rumors flying around as to where you went. I'm so sorry," she said with tears in her eyes. "I'm so sorry that I didn't fight harder to find you. Will you please forgive me?"

Casper wondered what his life would have been like if he was able to live with her after his parents died. Then he thought about Ryan.

What a difference having a will makes, he thought, taking a deep breath. He didn't bother to tell her how miserable his life had been; he figured it would only make her feel worse.

"Of course I forgive you," he said, as he gave her an appreciative smile.

Chapter 25

"Now, let's get you cleaned up so you can go see your parents," she said, standing up and leading him down the hallway to a room full of clothes sorted out by sizes. That should be your size over there," she said, pointing to a rack of men's clothes. "And the shower is right across the hallway."

"Okay, thanks."

It didn't take Casper long to find an outfit, but his shower was a totally different story. He took so long, the lady wondered if she should go in there to see if he was okay, but she could tell

that it had been a while since his body touched

water, so she left him in peace.

"Do you mind if I use one of the razors in

this pack?" Casper yelled.

"Sure, go ahead! There's also a new

toothbrush, toothpaste, and deodorant in the

basket under the sink. You can help yourself to

that as well," she mentioned.

She went back up front and waited

patiently for Casper to finish showering. While

she waited, her husband came and she excitedly

told him all about Casper being there. He

seemed just as enthusiastic as she was. He

tried to wait around for Casper to finish in the

bathroom, but he eventually gave up and told

his wife that he'd have to meet him later.

"Okay," she said to him, as she continued

to wait.

Finally, she heard the bathroom door open. When Casper walked into the room, she thought she was going to faint.

"My, my child! You sure do fix up nicely," she said. "Look at your face; it's as smooth as a baby's bottom. You look just like Gilbert Raine with all that hair off of your face," she said, still staring at Casper like she was in awe. "Are you ready to go?" she asked.

"Yes, ma'am. I sure am."

"Okay, well let's go," she said.

As they drove to the gravesite, Casper looked over at this woman who seemed to be an angel. She looked back at him with that radiantly flawless smile of hers.

"What's on your mind?" she asked him.

"I was just wondering why you moved

back here if you had moved to Pennsylvania."

The lady blushed, "Well, when I came down here to pay for your parents' burial, I met and fell madly in love with the Director of the funeral home," she said giggling.

Casper raised one of his eyebrows, and gave her a *you sly dog* look.

"It's not what you think," she reassured. "Well, maybe it is what you think," she laughed, "but to keep me from leaving, he offered me a job working with him, and he put me up in a hotel for two weeks. After that, he asked me to marry him, and I said 'Yes.'"

"After only knowing him for two weeks?"

"Well, when you know, you just know," she said, patting Casper on his shoulder.

He laughed out loud. "I guess," he said. "You seem to still be very much in love."

"Oh, I am. My first marriage was horrible, but this one is a match made in heaven," she said, going on and on, talking about the love of her life. She eventually stopped the car, looked over at Casper and said, "Well, we're at the gravesite now, so I guess I'll have to finish my story later. What time do you want me to come pick you up?"

"Pick me up?" he asked with a puzzled look on his face.

"Yes, you need somewhere to stay until you can get on your feet, don't you?"

"Yes, ma'am, I suppose I do, but I would really like to have a place of my own."

"Okay, well that can be arranged. How about you stay with us tonight, and tomorrow my husband will help you find a place to live? And if you need a job, we could definitely use your help at the funeral home," she added.

"Really?" Casper said like he was totally caught off guard. "Thank you! Umm, didn't you say earlier that my dad had money in an account for me?"

"Well, I know they opened a college fund for you when you were a few months old and your dad had money automatically going to the account each month. When I retired, it was still an active account. My husband or I will take you to the bank first thing in the morning to see if it's still there. Do you have any identification on you? You know they're not going to tell you anything without a proper I.D."

"Yeah, I still have my learner's license."

"Learner's license? Why haven't you gotten your permanent license?" she asked, but before he could answer she said, "Oh, nevermind, we will help you. No worries. Did you at least finish high school?"

"Ummm."

"Okay, we'll get that too, or at least help you get your GED," she said.

Casper tried to contain his excitement, but he couldn't. There was nothing containable inside of him right now. He saw his life finally making a turn for the better. "Thank you! I'm so speechless right now," he said.

"You're welcome. Casper, I wasn't able to help you when your parents died, and now I feel like I've being given a second chance. Just because you're an adult now, doesn't mean you don't still need a family to love you. I hope you will allow me and my husband to be your family."

As those words grazed over Casper's mind,

he immediately thought back to what Ryan said on the church steps. He hurried up and thanked her again, then jumped out of the car so she wouldn't see the tears in his eyes.

"I'll come to get you in two hours," she yelled.

"Okay," he said, quickly wiping his face and waving goodbye.

"Your parents' graves are all the way down on the left. They both have beautiful, white marble headstones. You can't miss them," she yelled as she slowly drove off.

"Okay, thank you," Casper said again, running in the direction where she was pointing.

Chapter 26

As Casper got closer to the grave with the white marbled headstones, he noticed a girl there, setting out flowers. He assumed she was the graveyard attendant.

"Thank you for keeping my parents' graves so beautiful," he said to her.

She looked up at him.

"Casper? Is that you?" she asked, then jumped into his arms like he was some superhero and she was his biggest fan.

"WHOA!!! Do I know—"

He paused, and took another look at her.

Then she smiled, showing off her crooked front tooth. Casper knew that tooth from anywhere.

"MARIA?" he screamed, holding onto her as tight as he could, then spinning her around.

"I can't believe it's you."

"No, I can't believe it's you," she said, kissing him on the cheek. They stood there holding each other, like there was nothing else in life that mattered.

"I missed you so much," he said.

She laughed, "Not even close to how much I've missed you."

They stood there, still holding onto each other, while Casper looked at how beautiful his parents' headstones were. He took a deep breath.

"Do you wanna go sit under that tree over there so we can catch up?" he asked.

"Sure."

"And how have you been?"

"I've been okay," Maria said.

"Just okay?"

"Yeah, just okay. My life took a turn for the worse when you left. It was horrific!"

"Yeah! Tell me about it!" he agreed.

"What do you mean? Your life was so perfect. How did it take a turn for the worse?" she asked, surprisingly.

When Casper told her the horrible life he had lived for the last few years, she burst into tears. "I can't believe that happened to you. You didn't deserve any of that. Is that why you walk with a small limp?"

"Yeah, but I'm alive, and all is well now. Enough about me, what happened with you?" Casper asked, trying to change the subject, so

Maria would stop crying.

"My life was equally as bad," she said. "When you left, my life ended. You know how abusive my mom was, but there was so much more going on that I never told you about. I was too embarrassed and I thought you would hate me. You were all I had, and I refused to take that chance."

"I could never hate you. I'm sorry you felt like you couldn't talk to me. What was going on."

Maria took a deep breath, and her face became cold and hardened.

"Ever since I was twelve years old, my mom made me have sex with my two brothers!"

"Manny and Miguel?" Casper asked, as his mouth fell open.

"Yes! They were only eleven and thirteen.

That explains the look they use to give when boys talked about Maria's body! he thought.

"I can't believe your mom would do such a thing to her children," Casper said.

"Yeah! Me either! She said she wanted to show them how to do it properly. My oldest brother used to vomit while we had sex. My youngest brother just looked confused, but eventually he started hating me, as if I was the reason this was happening to him. Within five months after you left, I got pregnant. I had no idea which one of my brothers fathered my child, but my mom said it was my youngest brother. I don't know how she could be so sure, but she seemed pretty adamant about it, like she was keeping record or something. My father knew this was going on, but he never stopped it. My

mom beat me the entire time I was pregnant. I
think she was trying to get me to miscarry, but I
didn't. I tried to make her happy so she would
stop doing bad things to me, but nothing helped.
She was a mentally sick woman, who
desperately needed help. When she drank, it
made her act worse, and she drank every waking
moment of the day. She made me drop out of
high school so no one would know that I was
pregnant. When I went to the hospital to have
my son, they saw all of the bruises on me and
immediately called Child Protective Services."

"Was her name, Ms. Holiday?" Casper
interrupted.

"No!" Maria said, frowning at him for
interrupting her story.

"I'm sorry. Please continue."

"Well, my youngest brother ended up

327

committing suicide while I was in the hospital and my oldest brother had a mental breakdown. He lives in a mental institution, now. He doesn't even know who I am when I go to visit him."

"Where is your son now?"

"He's in a special school that helps him with his speech and comprehension."

"What's wrong with him?"

"He was born with several deformities."

"So, you're taking care of him all by yourself?"

"No. I was adopted by a wonderful family and they are all helping me to raise him. It's like God finally shined down on me and surrounded me with people who love me.

"What happened to your parents?"

"They went to jail before my son was even born. The cops came and arrested my dad in the waiting room lobby and they took my mom

right out of the delivery room. I was so happy

they were gone, Casper. I didn't want either one

of them around my child. When the guys in jail

found out that my dad allowed my mom to do

that to us, they killed him. He wasn't even in

there a week. My mom is still alive, but she's

extremely violent and stays in solitary

confinement. She wrote me a letter one time

and told me she was sorry for everything she did

to me and my brothers, but I burned the letter

and stomped it in the ground, pretending that it

was her. You and your family were the only

people who were good to me. You guys really

loved me," Maria said slowly, as if something

had gotten caught in her throat.

"We still do love you," Casper said, then

paused. "Well, at least one of us does."

"I'm sorry that I didn't come back for you like I promised," he said sorrowfully.

Maria looked up at Casper and smiled. "You just did," she replied.

"I guess I did, huh?"

"Yup!"

"I would love to meet your son," he said.

"You would?"

"Yup."

She laughed, then laid her head on Casper's shoulder. He put his arms around her, and their world finally seemed perfect. They both stared off into the beautiful sunset. At that moment, Casper knew that God had answered Ryan's prayer.

The End

Meet The Author

I'm Colette Orr, founder of Orr Novels.

Writing is undoubtedly one of my favorite pastimes. When I first started writing, it wasn't because I wanted to sell a lot of books or because I wanted to become famous. I did it simply because I loved it. Of course I want people to buy my books and I want them to love them, but I often take myself back to my foundation, do it simply because you love it. If I never sell another book, I can honestly say I am content. This journey has far exceeded what I ever thought it would be. For that, I thank God and I thank you, my loyal readers.

My third book, *A Will To Live,* totally took me out of my comfort zone. It was exciting and thrilling to write and I hope it is equally exciting and thrilling to read. This is a topic that touches my core, because I wanted to address children who grew up in abusive homes. I wanted to tell the story from a child's point of view, but I didn't want to just write a book, I wanted to do more. For that reason, I'm committing to give a portion of this book's proceeds to organizations who help abused children. It is my way of saying, you're not forgotten. Thank you to everyone for your love and continued support. Words can't express my gratitude.

Colette D. Orr

www.ingramcontent.com/pod-product-compliance
Lightning Source LLC
Chambersburg PA
CBHW022002090426
42741CB00007B/859